Three Church Dramas

THREE CHURCH DRAMAS

by

OLOV HARTMAN

translated by

BRITA STENDAHL

FORTRESS PRESS

PHILADELPHIA

Translated from the Swedish
Tre Kyrkospel by Olov Hartman
Stockholm: Rabén & Sjögren, 1959

© 1966 by Fortress Press

Library of Congress Catalog Card Number 66-20516

3445F66   Printed in the U.S.A.   UB62P

Contents

Introduction

> A new form of religious drama has to be created from the old sources, from the old traditions and the old dramatic forms, from liturgy. Only in this way are we able to create a new religious drama which not only exists beside the real theater but seeks its own form.*

The three dramas presented in this book represent a church drama which seeks its own form. Its roots are not only in primitive biblical and liturgical forms, or in medieval sequences like the celebrated *Quem quaeritis* of the tenth century; its roots are also to be discovered in current forms of the church's theological and liturgical renewal and in recent insights of dramatic theory and practice.

The plays themselves are the product of a movement for church drama which was born at Sigtuna, Sweden, in 1953 with the presentation of *The Holy City*, a drama which celebrated the founding of that city more than nine hundred years ago. Out of that experience and as a result of co-operation between the writer and his principal stage director, Mr. Tuve Nyström, has evolved both a dramatic type of which the plays in this volume are

*From an address given at the World Conference on Religious Drama in Royaumont, France, in 1960.

vii

representative, and a movement for drama and liturgy in which several thousand persons have participated. The three plays to be found here date from 1954, 1956 and 1958. They are now presented for the first time in English in order to be taken, adapted, produced and experienced by an even wider circle of worshiping congregations.

This introduction is intended briefly to describe some of the principles underlying this form of church art and to supply certain guidelines for production.

A CHURCH ACTIVITY

In contrast to a considerable body of "religious drama" or "chancel drama" which we associate with the church building, church drama presupposes the co-operation of a worshiping congregation which is something quite other than a body of observers who happen to be present in the pews of the church. The presence of a worshiping congregation is, indeed, a theological necessity. We are not here dealing with a method of illustrating or explaining the word of God, like a Sunday school flannelgraph or a list of supplementary readings. Even less are we dealing with a method for infusing new life into a spiritless parish, or for awakening public curiosity, or for interesting theatergoers in the church. Church drama is art in the service of a message—a general characteristic it shares with the work of, say, Berthold Brecht. Since, however, church drama is *in the service of the Christian message,* its distinctive aim is to proclaim God's word to the congregation and to express the congregation's intercessions before God.

Nothing may stand in the way of this service. Artistic forms such as renaissance sculpture, baroque painting, and the music of romanticism all tend toward a self-expressionism alien to church drama. In sharp contrast, we here make no use of theatrical effects, suggestive colors, or even expressive music. It is to be the altar or the communion table, i.e., the prevalent symbol of God's presence in the midst of his congregation, which is to govern the worship and the drama. The identity between congregation and players, the use of hymns, the praying of the Our Father, the addressing of prayers toward the altar—all of these practices demonstrate the intimate relationship between drama and worship which these plays presuppose.

This view of drama and worship as proclamation and intercession faithfully reflects the character of much of the Bible. Not only do we secure material for these plays from the Bible; we endeavor to re-establish the relation between cult and drama which is basic to Christian worship and which, indeed, lies behind considerable sections of Scripture. For instance, recent investigation has demonstrated that many of the Psalms, hymns of the Old Testament congregation, can be understood only against the background of a cultic drama in which the figure of the king took on sacral significance. Or again, the meal of the Paschal Lamb must itself be seen as a cultic drama which sums up the entire history of God's people from Abraham to the Messiah. Church drama depends upon the restoration of this relationship between cult and drama. It seeks to re-establish the word of God as a dialogue in which God speaks to the world and the world to God. Through proclamation and intercession, made by dramatic action into visible signs, this dialogue is made manifest.

It is important, however, to warn against treating church drama as plays which "dramatize the Bible." In the sweep of creation, fall, salvation and consummation we have the very manuscript for the cosmic drama and the revelation of world and personal history as an action. Church drama is not something external which is applied to the Bible; church drama rather invests biblical actions and words with a dimension which they actually possessed from the beginning.

In summary, we may point to the faith that Christ is now present in the worshiping congregation as the theological and biblical keystone for church drama. This drama does not deal simply with something that has happened already or will happen at another time; this drama occurs here and now, involving the worshiping congregation immediately and not borrowing its reality from any other source. Consequently, it follows that church drama never allows Christ to be represented in the person of one of the players. No one is allowed to draw attention to himself and away from the one who is present in his word and in his sacrament. To portray Christ would be to hide the image of him which we possess in the sacramental act, to destroy the only authentic portrayal of Christ we have. Church drama thus constantly turns toward the altar (or the table or the pulpit, depending on the architectural and liturgical tradition of the worshiping congregation) both as the visible sign of Christ's immediate presence and as the door through which the worshiping congregation expects his return.

PRODUCING THE PLAYS

The fact that the plays found in this volume originated in the liturgical and architectural tradition of the Church of Sweden ought in no way to inhibit their production in the vastly different milieu of many English-speaking churches. A certain amount of inventiveness will be required, to be sure, depending upon the worship customs of particular churches, but the ecumenical character of the plays permits production within any tradition. In the following paragraphs an attempt will be made to point to certain features of these plays which will require care and imagination if successful productions are to result.

ALTAR. These dramas presuppose a focus of attention to which the action constantly makes reference. In many churches this will be the altar or communion table, and the designation used in this volume is that of the altar. In some churches, however, the pulpit or open Bible or a simple, naked cross will provide this center of attention. Obviously, this is to be the focal point for the congregation's worship as well as for the players' action.

The supposition in these plays is that at moments of prayer, the congregation, the players and the clergyman (where called for) will face in the same direction, namely, toward the altar. In churches which practice a different form of prayer—for example, where the one who leads faces the congregation or where a circle is the most natural expression of the fellowship of prayer—it is recommended that these directions be translated into closer conformity with the traditions of the congregation which is at worship.

Where antependia or other altar or pulpit hangings are

used to mark different seasons of the church year or different occasions for worship, it is an easy thing to fit such usage into these dramas. The appropriate color will usually be determined by the current season of the church year; at some points, however (e.g., in *Prophet and Carpenter*, Act Two), a change in color will be desired to mark a change in the action of the play. Similar principles should guide the use of candles, flowers, etc. Spotlights should be used in these plays only to aid the vision of the congregation and never to create special "dramatic effects."

ARCHITECTURAL GEOGRAPHY. In accordance with traditional symbolism, these plays locate the altar in the "eastern" end of the church, the so-called "liturgical east." In certain dramas, then, this geography preserves an ancient and helpful symbolism. For example, in *The Fiery Furnace* the north side of the chancel represents the place of the godless state, and the character Demas deserts the church for this state by moving from the south (the congregation's right) to the north. Another example of this use of architectural geography is to be found in *The Crown of Life* where, as in medieval mystery plays, the chancel and the nave together constitute an *imago mundi*, an image of human existence. Paradise is in the far east, at the altar, while the place of destruction is in the far west, toward the narthex. Further, in this play the north side represents the place of darkness and thus is the position of the Black Choir, which actively engages the White Choir, located in the south which is the place of light, in a battle symbolic of the struggle between good and evil.

COSTUMES OR VESTMENTS. In churches where the alb, the surplice and the cope are used as part of the liturgical tradition, it has been discovered that these vestments lend themselves admirably to use as costumes for church drama. The cope, for example, is well suited to players representing persons of rank; the alb may always be worn by angels and often by other choir members. By the use of symbolic colors and appliqués, costumes may be used to distinguish different roles and, on occasion, even different dramatic situations.

In circumstances where the traditional liturgical vestments are not used, it is entirely possible to pattern the dramas' costumes after garb customarily worn by laymen in the church's service—e.g., choir robes. Furthermore, there is nothing to prevent the players from creating a special form of costume appropriate to worship, which will indicate their special service to both the congregation and the drama.

While there is no need in church drama for properties, in certain instances the players are to carry implements which either identify their roles or enhance the action. Thus, a processional cross carried in *Prophet and Carpenter* can also serve as the mast of the ship, and the four beasts in *The Fiery Furnace* mark their traditional points near the altar by their staves to which the characteristic emblems—man, lion, ox, eagle—are affixed.

DRAMATIC ACTION. The players ought to enter the church in procession during the congregation's opening hymn. When their presence at the point of action is not called for, they should take places in the choir or with the congregation. The players are not required to make dramatic entrances or exits; they leave the church in a body at the conclusion of the service.

Inasmuch as these dramas are marked by a definite anti-expressionistic character, little movement, gesture or inflection should be employed. Careful blocking will allow the players to speak with directness and clarity. Stylized movement will suggest what is desired. For example, in *Prophet and Carpenter* a slight unison swaying at the knees by the captain and the sailors is sufficient to indicate the violent seas and need not be complemented by unseemly sound effects or programmatic organ music.

Similarly, care must be taken to avoid an artificial use of the speaking voice either by individual players or by the various choirs. The prayerful—almost liturgical—character of many of the speeches, especially those of the choruses, lends itself to the frequent use of chants or intonation. There are countless opportunities in these dramas for the creation of original liturgical music.

There are also in these dramas occasions for the development of pantomime and dance at points where the usual expectations of an "audience" would be otherwise. A pantomime, for instance, can eliminate the necessity for unwanted properties—e.g., the bow and arrow or the gourd required in *Prophet and Carpenter*. Similarly, for the second act of the same play it is possible to create an unobtrusive dance to portray the meaninglessness of the "Kingdom of Death": the inhabitants of this kingdom may move slowly toward each other, only to turn aside at the point where they should meet to wander toward a goal never reached. Such a dance conveys the impossibility of communication in the Kingdom of Death without distracting the congregation's attention from the actions of the prophet Jonah.

In all of these matters concerning the actual production of church dramas it is wise to remember that the church here as always speaks as "a voice crying in the wilderness." We are not striving for any particular aesthetic effect, we seek only to stand in the service of the words of proclamation and intercession.

HYMNS. An essential element in the co-operation between the players and the congregation is the singing of hymns which express the significance of the plays as worship. The hymns which are printed with the dramas in this volume are of course not prescriptive. They have been chosen to illustrate what is desired by way of congregational singing; if other hymns are selected they should faithfully reflect both the meaning of the drama and the parish's tradition of worship. The hymns included in this volume are frequently divided into stanza groupings to be sung at different points in the plays. These hymns, and their melodies, are as follows:

PROPHET AND CARPENTER
   " 'Welcome, Happy Morning!' Age to Age Shall Say" (Melody: *Fortunatus*)

THE CROWN OF LIFE
   "How Marvelous God's Greatness" (Melody: *Blomstertid*)
   "Thy Word, O Lord, Like Gentle Dews," Stanzas 2 and 3 only (Melody: *St. Matthew*)
   "Of the Father's Love Begotten" (Melody: *Divinum Mysterium [Corde Natus ex Parentis]*)

THE FIERY FURNACE
   "Holy, Holy, Holy, Lord God Almighty!" (Melody: *Nicaea*)
   "For All the Saints" (Melody: *Sine Nomine*)

ABOUT THESE PLAYS

The following paragraphs are offered as brief notes concerning the action and meaning of the plays included in this volume.

Prophet and Carpenter

In this drama, Jonah, on one level, is a disobedient prophet, numbered among the many pious individuals for whom a radical gospel of God's grace is an unwelcome and incomprehensible part of the biblical tradition; the distinction between the saved and the damned is for him one of the basic principles of existence. On this level the carpenter is simply a carpenter in Nineveh who—like the captain and the sailors—is bound to the rules of his vocation. The sea is the sea, the ship is the ship, Nineveh is Nineveh.

On another level the events of this drama make transparent a different pattern. The desperate atmosphere of Act Two, for instance, parallels the Old Testament's interpretation of the Kingdom of Death. Jonah's visit, however, foreshadows the visit of a greater prophet, descended into hell, on the third day to be raised from the dead. At other points as well this perspective breaks into the action, as when the tired prophet sleeps in the depths of the ship, when he is cast into the sea, when like one resurrected he appears in Nineveh and preaches repentance. Similarly, the carpenter is an archetype for another carpenter in that he repairs what has been broken and goes into the great city instead of away from it. On this level the ship is not merely a ship and Nineveh is not

Prophet and Carpenter, Act One

The CAPTAIN and the SAILORS.

"Quell thy people that rage against us, have mercy!"

First Presbyterian Church, Stamford, Connecticut

The Crown of Life, Act One

SATAN and ISA

"All these things will I give you . . ."

Holy Trinity Church, Uppsala, Sweden

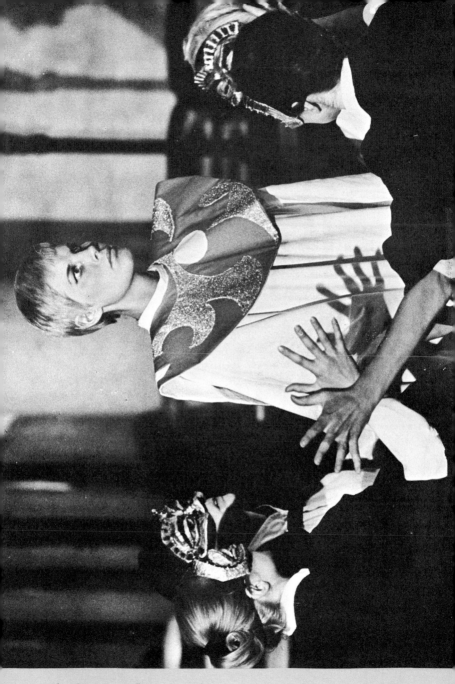

The Crown of Life, Act Two

ISA and the BLACK CHOIR

"The Queen of Paradise is captive . . ."

Engelbrekts Church, Stockholm, Sweden

The Fiery Furnace, Act Three

THE CAPTAINS and BABEL

"And the woman was arrayed in
purple and scarlet . . ."

The Sigtuna Foundation, Sigtuna, Sweden

merely Nineveh. We all sail in this ship and we all live in that city.

The Crown of Life

While the substance of this story is taken from the Genesis accounts of creation and the fall, into which themes from Job, the Psalms and various apocalyptic writings are woven, there stand behind the action certain conscious parallels to the New Testament. In Act One, Adam appears as a parallel to the Last Adam, Christ. In Act Two, there is a correspondence between Adam's temptation and Christ's temptation in the desert. Adam's rejection of the call to be a "Christ to his neighbor" leads in Act Three to a consideration of the most serious sin of all men, that which we might call the "anti-Christlike." Moving alongside these motifs is a theme stressing the relation between Eve and Mary, making it natural for the play to culminate in the Magnificat.

The Fiery Furnace

This drama is a synthesis of Revelation's account of the Lamb opening the seven seals and the description in Daniel of an encounter between a heathen dictator and the Israel of God. The time of the drama is the end (Matthew 24:14), and its location is the axis between heaven, marked by the four beasts at the altar, and earth, marked by the struggle between the worldly powers and the church of the faithful.

No great leap of the imagination is required to place the worshiping congregation in the midst of this play. The dilemma posed by a state which has "disinfected" the church to a harmless entity, the risk of a proclamation of judgment and forgiveness, the demands of loving care for the poor of the world—these are perennial issues facing Christian people. When the whole of humanity is cast into the fiery furnace, God hears the prayer of Daughter Zion and Christ returns. Then the congregation joins Shadrach, Meshach and Abednego in their song of praise.

Let me, finally, express personal appreciation to two individuals who have been instrumental in bringing these dramas to their present English form: to Mrs. Brita Stendahl of Cambridge, Massachusetts, who has not only translated the plays from their original Swedish but who has also assisted in the translation of the idea of church drama into an American idiom; and to Robert E. Seaver, Professor of Speech and Drama at Union Theological Seminary, New York, New York, who arranged for me to visit the United States in 1965 in order to consult with persons concerned about church drama and who has continued to assist in the preparation of these plays for publication.

OLOV HARTMAN

Sigtuna, Sweden
Pentecost, 1966

PROPHET AND CARPENTER

Players

JONAH, PROPHET	AMOS, PROPHET
THE CAPTAIN	QUEEN JEZEBEL
THREE SAILORS	THE CARPENTER
A MERCHANT	NINEVITE MEN
KING SAUL	NINEVITE WOMAN
KING DAVID	CHOIR

Act One takes place on a ship on the Mediterranean Sea.
  The church is the ship.
Act Two takes place on the same day in the Kingdom of Death ("the belly of the fish").
  The church is the Kingdom of Death.
Act Three takes place six weeks later on a mountain outside Nineveh.
  The church is this mountain and Nineveh.

Costumes:
  Jonah wears a purple robe made like an alb with a hood.
  The captain wears an alb and cape.
  The sailors wear surplices with appliquéd anchors.
  Saul, David, and Jezebel wear gray robes.
  Amos wears a gray alb and carries a shepherd's staff.
  The carpenter wears an alb.
  The Ninevites wear black albs.
  The choir wears albs.

Act One

[*The altar and pulpit hangings are in accordance with the season of the church year. The altar candles are lighted. After an organ prelude the actors except Jonah walk through the church up to the chancel. The sailors carry a mast formed like a cross.*]

HYMN [*congregation*]:

"Welcome, happy morning!" age to age shall say,
"Hell today is vanquished, heaven is won today!"
Lo! the dead is living, God for evermore!
Him, their true Creator, all his works adore.
   "Welcome, happy morning!" age to age shall say.

[*The* PLAYERS *for Acts Two and Three take their places in the pews as does the* MERCHANT. *The* CAPTAIN *and the* SAILORS *raise the mast in the chancel and find their places. The* CHOIR *stands along the sides of the chancel.*]

CHORUS:

The sail was red in the evening
we sailed westward in the sun-street
but black grass grew between the rocks
over golden stones of that street fluttered
all thy swelling billows.

SAILOR 1: The starboard deals are bulging, captain.

CAPTAIN: Tie ropes around her.

SAILOR 1: Aye, aye, sir. [*He shouts out into the congregation.*] Tie ropes around her.

3

CHORUS:

> The night's heavy wind
> awoke Death from deepest deep
> he flogs the water with his fins
> his wrath is foaming white over the widths
> the ship is shaking in the whirl
> where for his booty he's beating
> all thy swelling billows.

SAILOR 2: She cannot stand against the wind any longer, captain.

CAPTAIN: I see it; cast the drift-anchor.

SAILOR 2: Cast drift-anchor.

SAILOR 3 [*shouts out into the church*]: Cast drift-anchor.

SAILOR 1: The water is gaining, captain.

CAPTAIN: Let the oarsmen bail.

SAILOR 1: The water is still gaining, captain.

CAPTAIN: Let the cargo go.

MERCHANT [*from a pew in the church*]: But all my costly carpets, captain.

CAPTAIN: Let the cargo go.

MERCHANT: But the spices, the balm, the myrrh. . .

CAPTAIN: Let the cargo go.

MERCHANT: But the gold, captain, the gold, the gold.

CAPTAIN: Let the cargo go.

CHORUS:

> Neither sun nor stars
> but deep that calls unto deep
> and fear unto fear
> thou cast me into the deep
> into the midst of the seas
> and the waters compassed me about

4

why, why hast thou forsaken me
all thy swelling billows pass over me.

[*While the choir is singing the* SAILORS *gather around the
captain; they are confused and despairing.*]

SAILOR 1: Baal, Baal among clouds and fires, where is thy
power over the sea dragon? Baal, hero, have mercy!

ALL THREE SAILORS: Have mercy!

SAILOR 2: Isis, Isis, mother from afar, where is thy star?
Mother, light candles in thy windows, have mercy!

ALL THREE SAILORS: Have mercy!

SAILOR 3: Poseidon, Poseidon in the deep, where is thy
sceptre, the threefold one? Quell thy people that rage
against us, have mercy!

ALL THREE SAILORS: Have mercy!

CAPTAIN: The whole night long you have been calling to
those gods and how has it helped us?

SAILOR 1: Has it helped us to tie rope around the ship?

SAILOR 2: To cast the drift-anchor?

SAILOR 3: To let the oarsmen bail?

SAILOR 1: To let the cargo go?

CAPTAIN: Are all hands on deck?

SAILOR 1: Shall we throw the passengers overboard too?

CAPTAIN: Are all hands on deck?

SAILOR 1: Everyone but Jonah, captain.

CAPTAIN: Who is Jonah?

SAILOR 1: A Hebrew. He is fast asleep.

CAPTAIN: Asleep? In this storm?

SAILOR 2: Maybe he has no god.

SAILOR 3: Or maybe he is a god.

CAPTAIN: Get him.

SAILOR 3: Aye, aye, sir.

[SAILOR *3 goes to the back of the church seeking Jonah.*]

Chorus:

> Is it God who is asleep among us
> fallen down to our weariness
> leaning against the keel at the stern
> against the spine in the innermost parts of the
> ship
> the spine that is breaking between the sea and
> the sky
> while the ribs point
> toward downfalling darkness?

> Is it God who is asleep among us
> fallen down to our weariness
> leaning against the keel at the stern?
> Our weariness from before the beginning of
> the world—
> more secure than the unconscious foetus
> though she is already twisting in pestling pains
> and the child shall be cast into outer darkness
> where there shall be weeping and gnashing of
> teeth.

> Is it God who is asleep among us
> fallen down to our weariness
> leaning against the keel at the stern
> of the world which is creaking at its joints
> under the weight of heavens
> (passing away with great noise)
> now when all things are about to be dissolved
> and the nations call their gods void of counsel
> at the noise of the waves and the sea?

Is it God who is asleep among us
fallen down to our weariness
leaning against the keel at the stern?
Why do we cry to closed heavens?
God, in our weariness, our starless night
our vessel under ragged clouds
and silent eternities,
hast thou no concern whether we perish?

[SAILOR *3 brings* JONAH *up the aisle and into the chancel.*]

CAPTAIN: Are you Jonah?

JONAH: Jonah, Amittai's son, from Gat-Hahefer.

CAPTAIN: How can you sleep?

JONAH: Because I no longer have a God.

ALL THREE SAILORS: Then he *is* not a god.

CAPTAIN: No longer, you said?

JONAH: He wanted me to go to the east. I was to go east to preach.

CAPTAIN: And so you are going west?

JONAH: That's it. I've handed in my resignation, I am no longer on duty, I am going west. I can sleep now, why should I stay awake?

CAPTAIN: And why will you not go east?

JONAH: To the east? To Nineveh? —Because it was an insult.

SAILORS: An insult?

JONAH: Yes, to God-fearing prophets.

CAPTAIN: But why do you travel with us?

JONAH: To get away from my God.

CAPTAIN: And where do you live, you and your God?

JONAH: I am a Hebrew, and I fear the Lord, the God of heaven who made the sea and the dry land.

7

SAILORS [*afraid*]: Who made the sea!

CAPTAIN: No wonder it is storming.

JONAH: Is it storming?

SAILOR 1: He hasn't even noticed.

SAILOR 2: By Zeus, here is our scapegoat!

JONAH: Scapegoat?

SAILOR 3: Captain, let us find out if the storm comes from him. He has such a quiet conscience.

CAPTAIN: Very well. Maybe his conscience will wake up.

[SAILOR 3 *pantomimes aiming a bow and arrow upward.*]

SAILOR 2: Don't aim there. The arrow will fall down into the sea.

SAILOR 3: Then if it falls down before our feet the sign is still more certain. It is worth risking an arrow for a question of life and death.

[SAILOR 3 *shoots and everyone else stands aside in a circle. All look up, then turn to Jonah.*]

SAILOR 2: There it is, who does it point at?

SAILOR 1: Look here.

[ALL *rush over.*]

CAPTAIN: What have you done?

[JONAH *sees the storm.*]

JONAH: Do you mean it is storming because of me?

SAILORS: What have you done?

CAPTAIN: You said yourself your God made both the sky and the sea.

JONAH: Indeed. And he is no little idol from Japho—not to speak of the harlot of Nineveh.

CHORUS: What have you done?

JONAH: Why have you not forsaken me? I was comfortably asleep. Couldn't you allow me a little rest? Must you hunt me like game over land and sea, with your arrows?

CAPTAIN: What shall we do with you?

SAILORS: The sea is storming more and more.

JONAH: The storm is within me.

CAPTAIN: What shall we do with you, Jonah from Gat-Hahefer, to calm the sea?

JONAH: Take me up and cast me into the sea. Then it will be calm.

CAPTAIN: Take your places, we are swinging to. Let us see if she still obeys the helm.

[*The* SAILORS *scatter.*]

JONAH: Do you believe his wrath is so easily calmed?

CAPTAIN: If he is angry because you are going west, he is sure to calm down if we turn.

JONAH: I am not sure that my heart is turning.

CAPTAIN: I am not going to ask your heart for any help.

JONAH: You shouldn't neglect it—if I were to be persuaded.

CAPTAIN: And if I tried now, you would rather perish with us all than to turn your heart to the east.

JONAH: No, why should you all perish? I am enough. He will not be able to say that I am inhuman.

SAILOR 3: The larboard deals are bulging, captain.

CAPTAIN: That's what I thought, we cannot turn.

MERCHANT [*from a pew*]: The water is rising. We are finished. Damned gods that hear nothing.

CAPTAIN: What shall we do with you, Jonah from Gat-Hahefer?

JONAH: Take me up and cast me into the sea. He has made it storm because of me.

9

SAILOR 1: But what will he say if we drown his prophet?

JONAH: What did the arrow say?

CAPTAIN: Let us pray. Lord, let us not perish on account of this man's soul.

SAILORS: And lay not upon us innocent blood.

CAPTAIN: You yourself have decided it.

JONAH: You hear what they say? If you want to drown one of your best prophets, then let it happen. You are making an awful fuss—stirring up the whole sea because of me. But leave these poor Gentiles in peace. Amen.

[SAILOR *2 takes* JONAH *out through the aisle.*]

CAPTAIN: It is better that one man should die for the people than that all perish.

CHORUS:

> We discerned the face of the sky and said:
> a storm is coming, a storm and a tempest.
> But read to us the sign of the mast in clear
>   waters
> when the rags of the sail float from the beam
>   of the cross
> and the fish splash around the prow catching
>   glitters of sun.
> Who opened the mouth of the deep for his
>   servant
> and there was a great calm? Both the winds
>   and the sea
> obeyed him and he made all things new.
> We discerned the signs of the day and said
> the sky is red and lowering
> and tempests came and winds fell upon us.

10

Discern to us now when old things are passed,
discern to us the sign of Jonah in the belly of
    the ship
and the point of the arrow and the mouth of
    death,
discern to us the sign of Jonah in the deep
while the tar smells and the timber creaks in
    the sunshine
and seagulls cry out our questions over the sea.

HYMN [*congregation*]:
  Earth with joy confesses, clothing her for spring,
  All good gifts return with her returning King;
  Bloom in every meadow, leaves on every bough,
  Speak his sorrows ended, hail his triumph now.
    "Hell today is vanquished, heaven is won today!"

  Months in due succession, days of lengthening light,
  Hours and passing moments praise thee in their flight;
  Brightness of the morning, sky and fields and sea,
  Vanquisher of darkness, bring their praise to thee:
    "Welcome, happy morning!" age to age shall say.

[*The players of Act One sit down in the pews. The altar
candles and all chancel lights are extinguished for Act
Two. The hangings are changed to black.*]

11

Act Two

[*The door to the sacristy is closed; the mast lies on the floor representing a wreck.*]

CHORUS:
> Lord, who gives thee thanks in the Kingdom of
>   Death?
> What are thy works to him
> who has been swallowed by Leviathan?
> Here is no blooming summer, no scented wind.
> If armies overflow the earth and
> kingdoms are destroyed at their alarms,
> who will notice it in prison? Who will hear it
> among those who are swallowed by the deep?
> As fish in a sunken ship
> so travel kings and slaves in silence.
> What does he remember who himself is just a
>   memory?
> Whence walk the people that once were?
> Lord, who gives thee thanks in the Kingdom of
>   Death?

[*During these verses the gray crowd walk toward the chancel. They take dispersed places in the chancel, they do not see or hear each other, they stare at nothing. JONAH enters.*]

JONAH: He has finally given me peace—God is not here. [*Silence.*]

12

JONAH: I went to the west, away from his will. I thought
I fled from his presence. It was a miscalculation, I ad-
mit it, but now the mistake is corrected. He himself
has taken care of it.

SAUL: David, David!

JONAH: Oh, are you Saul? An honor for me to meet
the conqueror of the Philistines.

SAUL: David, play for me, David.

JONAH: Very noble of you to give David the honor he
deserves, though you are a little late. But tell me: I
have often thought of that Gentile you spared quite
against the prophetic command—Agag, I mean, the
king you should have stabbed until the blood splashed.
Nowadays you consider that slack policy a mistake,
don't you?

SAUL: David, play for me, play for me.

JONAH [*discovers David, who is an old man with hardly
the strength to sit up*]: Is it not David? Your Majesty,
receive my homage. Your kingdom is once again strong
as in your days, and it was I who prophesied it. With
a rod of iron are the heathen to be ruled.

DAVID: Abishag from Shunam, Abishag from Shunam.

JONAH: The girl who gave you warmth in your old age?
I am not quite sure—your sons had a little war about
her, you might say. There was some bloodshed but
when it quieted down Abishag disappeared from history. There have been conflicts of greater significance.

DAVID: Abishag, do not leave the old man, Abishag, Abishag.

JONAH: The kingdom is established, King David. It is
strong now and I was the one who prophesied it.

SAUL: David, play for me, David.

13

JONAH [*yells in the old man's ear*]: I prophesied your kingdom.

DAVID: Abishag from Shunam, Abishag, I am freezing.

JONAH: He does not hear a thing.

AMOS: Haoh! Haoh! Has anyone seen my sheep, a ram with white wool?

JONAH: Truly, here are people I longed to talk with. Amos, Amos, finally we meet. How could you? Just to come from your pastures in Judah and interfere with our affairs was matchless boldness. What has Jerusalem to do with Samaria? But to stand in Bethel itself and preach disaster! To discourage the hopeful ones and paralyze the confidence of the people!

AMOS: Haoh! Has anyone seen my sheep, a ram with white wool?

JONAH: You should have stayed in the mountains of Tekoa and devoted yourself to that sheep instead of getting involved in things that belong to kings and prophets. Or gone to the Gentiles with your trumpet of doom.

SAUL: David, play for me, play for me.

JONAH: But of course I had to go there—instead of reaping the harvest of my rightful prophecy. And my encouragement of Israel.

DAVID: Girl from Shunam, the old man is freezing.

JONAH: There came no doom, you see, Samaria is still standing and Bethel too. Do you hear that, old shepherd?

AMOS: Has anyone seen my sheep, a ram with white wool?

JONAH: [*turning to Jezebel*]: Why does none of them answer me?

14

[*Silence.*]

CHORUS:

> Here is no blooming summer, no scented wind.
> If armies overflow the earth and
> kingdoms are destroyed at their alarms,
> who will notice it in prison? Who will hear it
> among those who are swallowed by the deep?
> As fish in a sunken ship
> so travel kings and slaves
> in silence.

JONAH: Do you not answer either?

JEZEBEL: Naboth is dead.

JONAH: Jezebel, old witch! Yes, Naboth is dead, your enemy is dead. And we recognize you in his death, murderess. But you are also dead. The dogs ate you up.

JEZEBEL: Naboth is dead.

JONAH: Your children are dead too, every one of them. Jehu killed them, not a single one is left.

DAVID: I am freezing, I am freezing.

JONAH: And Baal is dead, Baal whom you worshiped. Your powerless idol. But the Lord lives in Bethel; there is the gate of heaven. You didn't know that, you Phoenician bitch, you thought the gate was at home, in Sidon.

SAUL: David, David.

JONAH: Don't think that it is because of any weakness for your debauched gods that I am refusing to obey the Holy One of Israel. On the contrary, what is wrong with him is that he is too good-natured to the mob— he ought to listen more to his prophets.

JEZEBEL: Naboth is dead.

15

JONAH: Naboth is dead, Naboth is dead, I know it. Can't you say anything else? You are like a talking bird—changed into a regular Egyptian death-god. Is this the death of the Kingdom of Death?

AMOS: Haoh! Haoh! Has no one seen my sheep, a ram with white wool?

JONAH: The prophet is dead, what is left is the shepherd.

SAUL: Play for me, play for me.

JONAH: The king is dead, but anxiety remains.

SAUL: David, David.

DAVID: Abishag, Abishag.

JONAH: They do not answer me. They do not even answer each other.

JEZEBEL: Naboth is dead.

JONAH: Like a thornbush sticking up out of burned ground does her evil deed live.

JEZEBEL: Naboth is dead.

JONAH: She is still telling her husband, but where is he?

AMOS: Has anyone seen my sheep?

JONAH: Everything else is sunk in the sea, in the depth of their death. As a city on the bottom of the sea where finally only one pillar, one gate, one gable of a temple rises out of the slime.

SAUL: David, David, play for me.

DAVID: Abishag, girl from Shunam, do not leave me.

JONAH: The name of a servant girl—an old man's hot-water bottle. This is what is left of David! What will be left of Jonah? Amos, do you hear me? Can't you answer a single word? Am I to become like these?

AMOS: Haoh! Haoh! Has anyone seen my sheep, a ram with white wool?

JEZEBEL: Naboth is dead.

16

JONAH: But if God is also dead, that does not concern you. Won't I be able to think of him either? Is he so far away that you cannot even deny him here? Jezebel, answer me, where is Israel's God?

SAUL: David, play for me, play for me.

JONAH: Yes, before death is through and loneliness completed, play for us, someone—for me, before it is too late.

DAVID: Abishag, Abishag, do not leave me, I am freezing.

JONAH: Truly, my escape has been too successful. His absence cries out of their silence and—I do not want, I do not want this loneliness, I do not . . .

[JONAH *runs to the door of the sacristy, pounds at it, tries in vain to break it down.*]

JONAH: The bars of the earth are about me for ever.

JEZEBEL: Naboth is dead.

SAUL: David, David.

JONAH: Lord, was it thou? I wanted to leave thee—was it thou, Lord, who determined my will? Was it thou who drove me away?

AMOS: Haoh! Has anyone seen my sheep? Haoh!

JONAH: I judged thee; didst thou judge me?

JEZEBEL: Naboth is dead.

DAVID: Abishag, Abishag, do not leave me.

JONAH: Thou hast cast me into the deep, into the midst of the seas, and the flood hast compassed me about, all thy billows and thy waves have passed over me.

CHORUS: The people that walk in darkness shall see a great light; they that dwell in the land of the shadow of death, upon them shall the light shine.

JONAH: My God, My God, why hast thou forsaken me?

17

[*Three heavy poundings on the door of the sacristy.* ALL *turn in that direction. Three more poundings.*]

JONAH: I am cast out of thy sight; yet I will look again toward thy holy temple.

[*Still three more poundings and the door is opened. A cone of light shines into the church.* JONAH *walks slowly toward the light and out into the sacristy.* ALL *stretch their arms toward the light and walk to their seats in the pews. During this time the* CHORUS *is speaking.*]

CHORUS:

> The Lord saith: I am the first and the last:
> I am he that liveth, and was dead;
> and behold, I am alive for evermore;
> and have the keys of hell and of death.

[*The* CHORUS *divides into two groups.*]

> I. Whither shall I go from thy spirit?
> or whither shall I flee from thy presence?
> II. If I ascend up into heaven, thou art there;
> if I make my bed in hell, behold, thou art there.
> I. If I take the wings of the morning and dwell in
> the uttermost parts of the sea;
> II. Even there shall thy hand lead me, and thy right
> hand shall hold me.
> I. And if I say: Surely the darkness shall cover me;
> even the night shall be light about me.
> II. Yea, the darkness hideth not from thee,
> but the night shineth as the day;
> the darkness and the light are both alike to thee.

> I, II. The Lord saith: I am the first and the last:
> I am he that liveth, and was dead;

18

and behold, I am alive for evermore;
and have the keys of hell and of death.

Hymn [*congregation*]:
  Maker and Redeemer, life and health of all,
  Thou from heaven beholding man's abasing fall,
  Of the Eternal Father true and only Son,
  Manhood to deliver, manhood didst put on:
    "Hell today is vanquished, heaven is won today!"

  Thou, of life the author, death didst undergo,
  Tread the path of darkness, saving strength to show;
  Come then, true and faithful, now fulfil thy word;
  'Tis thine own third morning; rise, O buried Lord!
    "Welcome, happy morning!" age to age shall say.

[*The altar candles and chancel lights are lighted and the
hangings are restored as they were in Act One.*]

19

Act Three

CHORUS:
> There shall no sign be given this generation
> but the sign of Jonah.

I. Thou ledst him out of the tomb and let him
pay what he had vowed "to preach unto Nineveh"
so he arose and went unto Nineveh
he cried and said "yet forty days, forty days."

II. Thou ledst him out of the tomb and in his doom
was a chill from the bottoms of the mountains
with the eye of the fish he saw our plantations
and his wrath that moved the ground
where we stood
was an angel's fever.

I. Thou ledst him out of the tomb, Lord, set him free
let him go
his shroud is a frost in sunheated streets
his life is a tomb for Nineveh—if not a sign.

II. Thou ledst him out of the tomb, O Lord—
if not a sign in the well of stars and
the parable of the fish
a sign of that which is more, which is more
than Jonah.

I, II. There shall no sign be given this generation
but the sign of Jonah.

[*The* CARPENTER *starts working on the mast.* JONAH *comes out of the sacristy. He stops at the stairs, holds his hand over his eyes, and looks out over the congregation.*]

JONAH: You can see the whole of Nineveh from here.

CARPENTER: Are you going there?

JONAH: Going there? Oh no, not today and not tomorrow either.

CARPENTER: It sounds as though you too believe that some calamity is about to happen. As do so many others.

JONAH: It was I who informed them that "some calamity" is about to happen.

CARPENTER: And now you will save your own life.

JONAH: I have done my share.

CARPENTER: Well, aren't you going home, then?

JONAH: First I want to see how it goes.

CARPENTER: And when shall it happen, your prophecy?

JONAH: Perhaps this evening, perhaps tonight, but tomorrow is the forty-first day.

CARPENTER: So, before sunrise.

JONAH: Before sunrise.

CARPENTER: Very well, you may stay if you like the place.

JONAH: It is very hot here.

CARPENTER: It will be hotter in Nineveh.

JONAH: What are you doing?

CARPENTER: Repairing a mast. There is a skipper here who would like to leave before it is too late.

JONAH [*examining the mast*]: It looks just like it!

CARPENTER: Do you understand such things?

21

JONAH: I too tried to sail away from Nineveh once, but I could not.

CARPENTER: The river is shallow at some spots—when it is dry like this.

JONAH: It was not on any river, it was on the Mediterranean.

CARPENTER: How can you sail away from Nineveh when you are on the Mediterranean?

JONAH: Didn't I say it was a failure?

CARPENTER: A strange way you must have travelled.

JONAH: It is hot here and there is no shade. The sun is beating on my head.

CARPENTER: Turn around and you will find shade.

[*In pantomime*, JONAH *catches sight of a gourd vine; he walks around it, wondering.*]

JONAH: This is the strangest thing I have ever experienced—no, perhaps not, but almost. Who are you, anyway?

CARPENTER: I? Don't you see I am a carpenter? I repair things that are broken.

JONAH: I mean, since there are such miracles about you.

CARPENTER: It is not over me that the gourd is growing. Sit down and get to know your value as a prophet.

JONAH: You are right, you are right. Such leaves and what a fragrance! A sign as good as any.

CARPENTER: Of what?

JONAH: That he has not forgotten me. He makes his sun rise on the evil and on the good but he has reserved the shade for the few. The judgment is over Nineveh, but here the blessing grows. The one goes with the other.

22

[*While Jonah is talking,* NINEVITES *are coming from the city. In pantomime, one bears a cracked cruse, another a cartwheel, another a wheatsheaf, another some ragged rugs; one woman is carrying her child in her arms. They are quite rash; one happens to tread on the gourd.*]

JONAH: No, no, no! What are you doing, man—tramping on the gourd, the nice gourd? What do you want here anyway?

FIRST NINEVITE: We want to stay close to you.

SECOND NINEVITE: For safety's sake.

JONAH: And why are you all dressed in black?

FIRST NINEVITE: Because the king has ordered it. Don't you know that the whole city is doing penance?

SECOND NINEVITE: And fasting. Even the mules and cows must fast.

JONAH: And what is that good for?

THIRD NINEVITE: To spare us from the doom.

NINEVITE WOMAN [*touches Jonah with curiosity*]: Is it true that you have been dead?

JONAH: Yes, that is true—and it is equally true that none of what I have predicted will be altered.

FIRST NINEVITE: Why did you say it?

JONAH: It was the condition for my escape from death. When I was finally vomited out on the shore of death, my Lord said, "Preach doom unto Nineveh."

SECOND NINEVITE: But what can we do?

JONAH: How do I know? My commission was to preach doom and I have done that now. What you shall do or not do is no concern of mine. I have never presumed to say anything about that.

FIRST NINEVITE: But if we repent?

JONAH: You are men of Nineveh all the same.

SECOND NINEVITE: We cannot help that, can we?

JONAH: If you could help it then your heathen abomination would be something you could grasp and handle, but now you are what you are. Snakes are snakes and weeds are weeds.

WOMAN: How is it to be dead?

JONAH: You already have its cadaverous smell. You are already dead to most things—down there is the grave of what you were. You there with the cruse and you with the wheel, and you with the rug and you with the sheaf—look what splinters of life you cling to. Soon even less will be left, less for you to keep in your hands, less for you to say, less for you to think. Until the last splinter of life sinks to the bottom.

WOMAN: But I have the child, I have the child.

JONAH: Get away with your damnéd child. What Israel's God has condemned I have no right to spare. Get away all of you, do you think I want to fall under the same condemnation as Saul when he saved King Agag?

FIRST NINEVITE: What if there is no doom coming?

JONAH: Yes, you may still doubt for a little while.

SECOND NINEVITE: What proof do we actually have?

WOMAN: He has been dead.

THIRD NINEVITE: How do we know?

JONAH: I say, go away.

FIRST NINEVITE: You don't want us to be here when the sun rises, do you?

JONAH: Never again will it rise over Nineveh.

THIRD NINEVITE: But if it does—you would prefer to be alone then.

FIRST NINEVITE: Are you afraid that we shall laugh at you?

JONAH: Very well, you may come here and spit in my face if the God of Israel has lied.

SECOND NINEVITE: We will remember that.

[*The* NINEVITES *slowly withdraw to the bottom chancel steps on the north side. Their heads lower as if they are falling asleep. Meanwhile the* CARPENTER *has removed "the gourd" (in pantomime).* JONAH *touches his head.*]

JONAH: How hot it is again [*looks up and finds that the gourd is not there*]. Now what is this?

CARPENTER [*comes forward and examines the plant*]: The neighborhood of death.

JONAH: Is it Nineveh that is about to be judged or is it I? I surely prefer the chilly death to the hot one. Is the stalk broken? It's the fault of that man from Nineveh who was tramping around here.

CARPENTER: Worms have eaten into the gourd.

JONAH: Worms? Worms? Surely I am not that dead, yet.

CARPENTER: The eggs must have already been here when the gourd first sprang from the ground.

JONAH: That is him all right.

CARPENTER: Who?

JONAH: The one who sees how one creature rejoices in another—and how death at that very moment is flitting around, laying eggs in the leaves. Sees it and allows it. No, sends it. And hands his servant over to everything that crawls and sneaks and creeps and gets that cadaverous smell here in the sun. I will not take part any more—he may take my life if he wants, I prefer dying to living in this Gehenna.

25

CARPENTER: For the gourd's sake?

JONAH: Is that not reason enough?

CARPENTER: But you did not labor for it, did you?

JONAH: No, what do you mean?

CARPENTER: And it was born and died on one and the same day.

JONAH: But don't you understand that one gets to like such a thing—it was like a blessing over the prophet's head.

CARPENTER: Just think if God, too, starts liking.

JONAH: The gourd?

CARPENTER: Nineveh.

JONAH: Nineveh?

CARPENTER: It is not just a gourd, that great city. It is an oak or a cedar, and how old might it be?

JONAH: I prefer the gourd that he killed.

CARPENTER: Furthermore—there are a hundred twenty thousand children in Nineveh.

JONAH: They too belong to Ham's damnéd race.

CARPENTER: And also much cattle. Even one or two gourds.

JONAH: Where are you going?

CARPENTER: The mast is ready now.

JONAH: But what about the doom?

CARPENTER: Then the skipper needs his mast that much more!

JONAH: But you yourself—what will happen to you?

CARPENTER: To me? Oh, I am no prophet—why should I be spared? I belong with them down there.

[*The* CARPENTER *walks down the aisle, carrying the mast like a cross on his back. He raises the cross in the middle*

26

of the congregation. At the top of the aisle, he turns around.]

CARPENTER: Look me up later on—after the doom. If you happen to have something that needs repair.

CHORUS:

  I. What do the hands of shadow seek, that feel the
        gables with stretching fingers
    while the sun-square is hunted still higher on the
    wall of the dark room
    and on the market place the white linen of day
    shrinks to a shroud for the respite?
    Why do the ants gather on the path?
    Why do the dogs sneak away from the city?
    Why do no swallows shriek over the well?
    What do the hands of shadow seek, that feel the
    gables with stretching fingers?

  II. O night! asleep without anticipation
    while the snake wriggles over the floor
    and the worm eats the root of the plant
    and death patrols the street like the watchman
    calling out the hours for our security.
    O night! asleep without anticipation.

WOMAN: Where is your wife?

FIRST NINEVITE: At home.

THIRD NINEVITE: Didn't she believe in the doom?

FIRST NINEVITE: Oh, yes, but not for us. "You can go," she said, "I'll stay home and watch the house."

WOMAN: How could you leave her?

FIRST NINEVITE: How could she stay when I went?

THIRD NINEVITE: Do you see where that light just came

on, straight to the north? No, not there, down there to the right. My parents lived there.

FIRST NINEVITE: Close to the library?

THIRD NINEVITE: As close to Nabu's temple. There was soft white sand in the yard. We boys used to sift the sand over our feet. Sometimes we lay on our backs in that soft white sand and looked up at the swallows.

SECOND NINEVITE: At home we had a fig tree that was good to eat from—when nobody caught us. It was good to climb too.

WOMAN: We had just paid off the mortgage on our little house.

THIRD NINEVITE: There is a well in the yard; it never runs dry.

WOMAN: And an apple tree at the well, where there is shade. I often sat there while I was expecting the child, it rested me.

FIRST NINEVITE: We had no children, but we had flowers on the roof and in the garden there was a lawn for a couple of sheep. But I wanted goats instead; we often quarreled about it.

WOMAN: Was it because of that she did not come with you?

FIRST NINEVITE: "Flowers and grass you can get every-where," I said. "Not these flowers and this grass and these sheep," was the answer I got.

THIRD NINEVITE: Strange that one sees so many lights down there.

SECOND NINEVITE: As dark as you think it is when you walk in the streets at night.

FIRST NINEVITE: Almost like a mirror of the starlit sky.

THIRD NINEVITE: With odd constellations that mean

28

something we do not understand. He who has judged us knows well what they mean, I suppose.

WOMAN: But he does not know how it is to sit in the shade at a well and see the sun filter through the crown of an apple tree. And have a child in one's arms.

SECOND NINEVITE: Nor how it is to count the buds of a fig tree when summer draws nigh.

FIRST NINEVITE: Nor to lie down in the sand and watch the birds in the sky.

THIRD NINEVITE: If he had seen you as you were just as the child was born! You were almost broken to pieces by the pains and you were completely hoarse—you had been screaming—but at the moment of the birth you smiled, you had forgotten everything and were only happy. And I could not speak; I thought it was so beautiful.

WOMAN: A man was born into the world, should not sorrow be turned into joy?

SECOND NINEVITE: What a thought—that Jonah's God would have noticed how a woman is when she is having a child.

WOMAN: Everything looks different from above, I guess.

THIRD NINEVITE: And now he is going to take it all and cast it against the rocks.

FIRST NINEVITE: The whole mirror of heaven, the stars and everything.

SECOND NINEVITE: If he does not let the stars fall down, like shaking a fig tree.

FIRST NINEVITE: Yes, why does heaven never fall down?

THIRD NINEVITE: Maybe it does . . . Now! Look—look there, there!

ALL: The doom comes, the doom, the doom comes over Nineveh.

JONAH [*who has been asleep during this conversation*]: What is it, where am I? I heard a cry—or did I dream it? Oh, it is the doom, it is the doom. Blessed be thou, Israel's God, who dost not abandon thy servant. Thou who dost let the mountains blacken like pest-boils on the face of the earth—thou who dost bloody the clouds with your sword which is drawn over that great city—that great city—now they remember in the narrow streets what Jonah said, they remember in the market places what the prophet preached, the Mighty One of Israel cannot lie. Look at the burning coals he rakes down over the earth from the oven of his wrath. The river is glowing like melted copper in the glare of thy fire coals, there is smoke over the plain where the burning stream runs through the grass. Blessed be thou, Lord of Judgment, blessed . . .

[*A moment of silence.*]

WOMAN: It is the sun!

THE MEN FROM NINEVEH: The sun, the sun.

WOMAN: A new day over the earth. And the apple tree is still standing at the well.

JONAH: As a fisherman puts his hook in the jaws of the fish, so hast thou dragged me, Lord. From death itself thou hast dragged me up and cast me on a sand shore; yes, like a fish that is gasping in the heat so am I before thee. Thou didst to me great things, but to make me a laughingstock thou didst lay thy words in my mouth only to betray them all; to plague me and to mock me hast thou clad me in the prophet's cloak, and now I have only this prayer left: Lord, come and take my life before they come and mock both thee and me—because they will spit in my face, Lord, they will hit me and say: "Prophesy who it was that smote you." —And is it not then thy face they spit upon, God of Israel?

[*The* Ninevites *start up the steps to the chancel.*]

JONAH: Hurry, Lord, hurry, they are coming, those who spit on thee. [*When the men of Nineveh are close to him.*] Where are your sticks and stones? Kill me first and mock me later.

FIRST NINEVITE: Why should we mock you?

JONAH: Because it did not happen as God's word had said.

FIRST NINEVITE: How could we know that? Maybe the judgment has fallen on someone else.

JONAH: Who? Who?

SECOND NINEVITE: We just want to thank you.

JONAH: Me? Why?

FIRST NINEVITE: Because someone must have prayed to your God for us. And who else could it be?

THIRD NINEVITE: We trampled on your gourd, but you did not trample on Nineveh.

WOMAN: We are so happy we can go home again.

FIRST NINEVITE: Where the doom is gone we do not know, but thank your God from us for this other thing —for his mercy. Since you have prayed for us.

JONAH: I know whom the doom has stricken.

THIRD NINEVITE: Who?

JONAH: Nineveh is on fire—in his heart.

FIRST NINEVITE: Can't you pray for him too?

31

JONAH: To think I have prayed for myself! Now everything is in pieces, broken like the mast he repaired. Carpenter, pray for me! Carpenter, pray also for me!

[ALL *turn to the altar. The* PLAYERS *from Acts One and Two join them in the chancel.*]

CHORUS:
    I, II. O, thou who dost capture us fleeing,
          making thyself a testimony out of our denial.
      I. What avails us the ship to Tarshish
         when the storm petrels are thy angels
         and the sail of our treachery is crossed
         by thy signs?
      II. What avails us the silence of hateful anguish
         from broken ships
         when our footsteps are a secret message
         that thou art coming soon
         and the doors of hell await thy key?
      I. What avails us the armor of obedience around
         our hearts?
         What refuge is the rock of piety
         when thou art so merciful in thy judgment
         and dost judge us so unsparingly in thy mercy?
    I, II. O, thou who dost bear us when the sea carries
         us and dost hide us close to thee when all else
         breaks away
         healing the broken mast with thy body
         sending the Gentiles to witness to thy servants
      I. Lord, have mercy upon us
      II. Christ, have mercy upon us
    I, II. Lord, have mercy upon us.

[*The pastor has proceeded to the altar.*]

The Our Father

The Benediction

Hymn [*congregation*]:

Loose the souls long prisoned, bound with Satan's
   chain;
All that now is fallen raise to life again;
Show thy face in brightness, bid the nations see;
Bring again our daylight; day returns with thee;
   "Hell today is vanquished, heaven is won today!"

Amen.

THE CROWN OF LIFE

Players

ISA, *later called* EVE

ADAM

SATAN

CHORUS *of angels*:
the WHITE CHOIR
and the BLACK CHOIR

READER *(Pastor or Layman)*

The play takes place in the chancel and on the steps up to the chancel. According to custom the chancel represents paradise or heaven and the altar is the throne of God. At the opening of the play all of the players are in the chancel; the three main actors come forth in turn from the choir stall.

Costumes:

The main actors and the choirs are dressed in surplices, albs or choir robes.

The members of the Black Choir also wear black robes or capes for the greater part of the play.

The "tree of knowledge", in the center of the chancel, ought not to be naturalistic; a large candlestick (minora) will do very well.

The altar and pulpit hangings are white until the end of Act Two, purple in Act Three until the Magnificat, then white.

The play can be shortened by omitting the choir parts which begin Act One and end Act Two.

Act One

HYMN [*congregation*]:

> How marvellous God's greatness,
>   How glorious his might,
> To this the world bears witness
>   In wonders day and night.
> In form of flower and snowflake,
>   In morn's resplendent birth,
> In afterglow at even,
>   In sky and sea and earth.
>
> Each tiny floweret whispers
>   The great Life-giver's Name;
> The mighty mountain masses
>   His majesty proclaim;
> The hollow vales are hymning
>   God's shelter for his own;
> The snow-capped peaks are pointing
>   To God's almighty throne.

CHORUS:

> In the beginning was the Word, and the Word was
>   with God, and the Word was God.
> The same was in the beginning with God.
> Who hath laid the measures of the earth? Or who
>   hath stretched the line upon it?

37

Whereupon are the foundations thereof fastened? or
who laid the cornerstone thereof;

When the morning stars sang together, and all the
sons of God shouted for joy?

Or who shut up the sea with doors when it brake
forth, as if it had issued out of the womb?

And had the cloud made the garment thereof, and
thick darkness a swaddling band for it?

In the beginning was the Word, and the Word was
with God, and the Word was God.

The same was in the beginning with God.

[*The* READER *goes to the altar with the Bible.*]

CHORUS:

All things were made by him; and without him was
not anything made that was made.

Hast thou commanded the morning since thy days;
and caused the dayspring to know his place;

That it might take hold of the ends of the earth?

It is turned as clay to the seal; and they stand as a
garment.

By what way is the light parted, which scattereth
the east wind upon the earth?

Who hath divided a watercourse for the overflowing
of waters, or a way for the lightning of thunder;

To cause it to rain on the earth, where no man is;
on the wilderness, wherein there is no man;

To satisfy the desolate and waste ground; and to
cause the bud of the tender herb to spring forth?

Hath the rain a father or who hath begotten the
drops of dew?

All things were made by him; and without him was
not anything made that was made.

READER: "And God said: Let us make man in our image, after our likeness: and let them have dominion over the fish of the sea, and over the fowl of the air, and over the cattle, and over all the earth, and over every creeping thing that creepeth upon the earth. So God created man in his own image, in the image of God created he him; male and female created he them. And God blessed them."

[ADAM *and* ISA *come before the altar holding hands like a bride and groom.*]

CHORUS:

> Love is of God; and everyone that loveth is born of God.
>
> When I consider thy heavens, the work of thy fingers, the moon and the stars, which thou hast ordained;
>
> What is man that thou art mindful of him? and the son of man, that thou visitest him?
>
> For thou hast made him a little lower than the angels, and hast crowned him with glory and honor.
>
> Love is of God; and everyone that loveth is born of God.

READER: "And the Lord God planted a garden eastward in Eden; and there he put the man whom he had formed. And out of the ground made the Lord God to grow every tree that is pleasant to the sight, and good for food; the tree of life also in the midst of the garden, and the tree of knowledge of good and evil. And the Lord God took the man and put him into the garden of Eden to dress it and to keep it."

[*The* CHOIR LEADERS *give burning candles to* ADAM *and* ISA, *who light the candles in the minora.*]

READER: "And the Lord God commanded the man, saying, Of every tree of the garden thou mayest freely eat: But of the tree of knowledge of good and evil, thou shalt not eat of it; for in the day that thou eatest thereof thou shalt surely die."

CHORUS:

> In him was life; and the life was the light of men.
> Thy faithfulness is unto all generations; thou hast
>   established the earth, and it abideth.
> They continue this day according to thine
>   ordinances: for all are thy servants.
> I have seen an end of all perfection: but thy
>   commandment is exceeding broad.
> In him was life; and the life was the light of men.

READER: "And there was war in heaven; Michael and his angels fought against the dragon; and the dragon fought, and his angels."

[*The* CHORUS *divides. The* BLACK CHOIR *take their robes over their arms and turn toward the altar.* SATAN *does likewise. He prays:*]

SATAN: O Lord of heaven and earth, we, who are about to give voice and shape to that darkness for which no one may pray and with which no one may unite, beseech thee to preserve us in our faith and our prayer so that we then may lay aside the guise of the enemy with thanksgiving, and praise thee in the reality thou givest to thy church on earth; through Jesus Christ, our Lord.

BLACK CHOIR: Amen.

[SATAN *and the* BLACK CHOIR *put on their black robes.*]

SATAN: What is the Almighty?

BLACK CHOIR: That we should serve him? And what profits should we have, if we pray unto him?

WHITE CHOIR:

> As he loved cursing, so let it come unto him: as he delighted not in blessing, so let it be far from him.
>
> As he clothed himself with cursing like as with his garments, so let it come into his bowels like water, and like oil into his bones.
>
> Let it be unto him as the garment which covereth him, and for a girdle wherewith he is girded continually.

ISA: Who are you?

SATAN: The angel of light.

ISA: You more than the others?

SATAN: For me there are no others. But who are you?

ISA: I am Isa.

SATAN: Who named you Isa?

ISA: Don't you know that Adam gives names to everything?

SATAN: I am a stranger here.

ISA: God doesn't seem to think the creatures really exist until Adam has seen them and said something.

SATAN: Who is Adam?

ISA: You are the first angel I've met who doesn't know who Adam is. He was the first of us two, and we are the image of God. God said so.

SATAN: I've heard about that. I've heard that the flesh is valued far more than the spirit.

ISA: I don't understand.

SATAN: How could you, a being of the dust of the ground, understand me? All the same he prefers this dust to the angels.

BLACK CHOIR: He prefers the dust.

WHITE CHOIR: Amen: Blessing and glory, and wisdom, and thanksgiving, and honor, and power, and might, be unto our God for ever and ever. Amen.

ISA: Look how many have already gathered.

SATAN: What are they doing here?

ISA: Oh, I thought you had come to join.

SATAN: Join?—A word for slaves.

BLACK CHOIR: Amen: Blessing and glory, and wisdom, and thanksgiving, and honor, and power, and might, be unto our God for ever and ever. Amen.

SATAN: What are they doing here?

ISA: They wait for the sun to set.

SATAN: But they turn to the east.

ISA: Yes . . . more than they that watch for the morning.

WHITE CHOIR: My soul waiteth for the Lord.

ISA: And when the wellspring of life has become black under the great mountain in the west, black with white flares of angels and seagulls, then suddenly there appears a multitude of the heavenly host, and in the high places there is thunder from their wings and the wellspring gleams as at sunrise. But after a little while there is a great silence and a great darkness, because the angels hide their faces. I wonder why they do that when God appears? Do you know?

SATAN: I do. That is why I will never do it.

WHITE CHOIR: Thou shalt worship the Lord, thy God.

BLACK CHOIR: We have no other king than Caesar.

[ISA's *eyes follow a serpent on the ground.*]

ISA: Look at that animal, so funny and so pretty. Like a silver brook running through the grass—no, now it is red! Now it is green! It plays with colors like the mirror of a lake.—Beautiful brook, where are you running?—Surely he will join us and get his name tonight. I wonder what Adam will call him.

SATAN: *You* name him something.

ISA: I can't. Adam is the one who is helping God to create. God has given the beings their eyes, ears and all members. Adam gives them their names. Then they are fully created.

SATAN: So I am not yet fully created.

ISA: Are you among those over whom we rule? Are you perhaps a bird? God said, "Have dominion over the fish of the sea, and over the birds of the air, and over every living thing that moves upon the earth."

BLACK CHOIR: What is man?

WHITE CHOIR: Thou hast made him a little lower than the angels.

ISA: He must take a good look at them, too. It is just as important that they be in his eyes as in the sea or in the air or on the ground.

SATAN: And if they are in my eyes?

ISA: In your eyes? Is it possible to be in them?

43

SATAN: Not everybody can live in fire.

ISA: I really did not exist until Adam had seen me and said: "Isa." How could I be Isa if he hadn't seen me and called me Isa? He said just that: "Isa."

SATAN: Woman.

ISA: I have him in myself. "Is": that is man. "Isa"—that's ... Isa. It is a feeling like dew in my hair when I wake up in sunshine.

SATAN: Why are you so content with dew when there are stars?

ISA: What do you want from me?

SATAN: I want to give you your crown, your crown of stars.

ISA: But I have it already. Adam told me so one night when it was quiet and the sky shone above us.

SATAN: What power did you get from those stars, woman? Adam keeps the garden, Adam creates, Adam talks with heaven and the angels—I know very well that I am the first angel *you* have ever talked with.

ISA: But I talk all the time with Adam.

SATAN: Even though you have your final name and star, you are outside.

ISA: Outside? Is the earth outside when the rain is falling from the sky? Is a woman outside when a man gives his seed to her? Or when he writes his poems in her heart?

SATAN: What a world!

BLACK CHOIR:

> To be in the heart of man
> making poetry of blue flowers,

44

> no burning coals or anxiety,
> no loneliness or power!

ISA: And in the morning there is a clear drop of dew in the leaves because heaven loves the earth and God is all in all.

WHITE CHOIR: God is all in all.

SATAN: And nobody is anything in himself.

BLACK CHOIR:

> Where are the dark spheres?
> Where is distance, hatred, terror,
> the arc which falls from star to star,
> from abyss to abyss?

ISA: Abyss? I know what that is. The place where the water of life throws itself down from the spring-lake. The place where the rock has burst and deep calls unto deep.

WHITE CHOIR: Now deep calleth unto deep.

BLACK CHOIR: Where are the dark spheres?

WHITE CHOIR: God is love. How could *he* be loneliness?

ISA: It was not good for the man to be alone.

WHITE CHOIR: How could he then be the image of God?

ISA: And the Lord God caused a deep sleep to fall upon Adam.

BLACK CHOIR: Surely we shall not die!

WHITE CHOIR: And darkness was upon the face of the deep.

ISA: So he fell into the hands of God and was no longer himself. Man burst, and the Lord God built a woman from the rib he had taken.

WHITE CHOIR: There shall be no more loneliness.

ISA: Adam has a scar on his side. I wonder if it is absolutely certain that it will never break open again.

WHITE CHOIR: Greater love hath no man than this, that a man lay down his life.

BLACK CHOIR:

> Where are the dark spheres?
> Where is distance, hatred, terror,
> the arc which falls from star to star,
> from abyss to abyss?

ISA: And when I looked down into the deep where the wellspring of life looses itself, I knew what "abyss" means, how man bursts into unity, and how Adam loves Isa and is loved in return.

WHITE CHOIR: Rock of ages, cleft . . .

ISA: Deep calls unto deep.

SATAN: You call that the abyss? I'll tell you something. The abyss does not call, it is silent. There is no bottom. What falls down, falls down into silence.

ISA: Poor you!

SATAN: Have you understood so little that you have pity on the power?

ISA: Which power?

BLACK CHOIR: You heard the blasphemy!

WHITE CHOIR: Which power?

SATAN: A crown of stars. All the kingdoms of the world and their glory. All these things will I give you if you fall down and worship me.

ISA: All the kingdoms of the world! Adam! Adam!

ADAM: Isa?

ISA: There is an angel here who does not know what you have given to me.

ADAM: What God has prepared for those who love.

ISA: Let us go to the high mountain and let me wear my crown.

ADAM: Look!

ISA: Ridges far away. Deep down, waves of green foam.

ADAM: And the eye of the lands, the wellspring of the rivers, black in the shadow of the mountain.

ISA: Heaven looks at us from earth.

ADAM: Earth looks at us through the sun of heaven, a glowing pupil in the deep.

WHITE CHOIR: What then is heaven? What then is earth?

BLACK CHOIR: Power!

WHITE CHOIR: Love!

ADAM: What then is man? And what is woman?

ISA: What is high up? And what is low down?

SATAN: If thou be the lord of the deep, cast thyself down.

BLACK CHOIR: Surely we shall not die!

[ADAM and ISA turn and look at each other.]

ISA: You did cast yourself down into the deep.

ADAM: Yes, into God.

ISA: To surrender yourself, not anticipating resurrection from that heavy sleep.

WHITE CHOIR: Which the anti-being calls dying.

ADAM: God calls it loving.

ISA: And living.

SATAN: But it is to surrender. You could have forced the angels to carry you, but you chose to burst and become two forever condemned to be slaves to each other.

BLACK CHOIR: Why should we die?

ISA: In love like all others.

WHITE CHOIR:
> Like a drop of blood
> the strawberry humbly bends its stem
> for the hungry.
> Like God's flower of fire
> the sun proudly gives its golden treasure
> to the dust
> which answers with buttercups
> and scarlet red mushrooms.

ISA: In love.

WHITE CHOIR: God is love and he that dwelleth in love dwelleth in God, and God in him.

BLACK CHOIR: Our Lord is loneliness and he that dwelleth in loneliness dwelleth in our Lord, and our Lord in him.

SATAN: Surely you shall not die.

WHITE CHOIR:
> He that loseth his life shall find it.
> Behold the water of life in the spring-lake, open to the steep whose crest, clear as glass, vaults like the skies of night and casts itself down, breaking into thousands of suns, and the ground beneath trembles at the white noise.
> The cleft roars with open jaws, the snake-jaws of the four rivers, the ever-thirsting gorge of

forests, the tomb where God's well dies to give
the world life in resurrection.
The well of God has water to the full.
He that loseth his life shall find it.

ISA: Satan, what do you know about love?

SATAN: That it is blind to what happens around it.

ADAM: The creatures are gathering, the fish draw the
bow of the sun on the water, the birds cry over the
reed and the ground is moving under the cloven hoofs
of the cattle.

ISA: And the angels are already shaking the skies.

SATAN: But one creature you forgot to name. Here is
the edge of your power. And you shall not find its
name to call it back until I have taken seven other
spirits with me and have entered to dwell therein.

ISA: The silver brook in the grass!

ADAM: Like gold shines the lake of Havilah. Let us be
prepared. God will surely find the silver brook.

[Silence.]

[ALL *suddenly kneel facing the altar except* SATAN *and
the* BLACK CHOIR, *who turn away.*]

WHITE CHOIR:

Holy, Holy, Holy, is the Lord of Hosts!
The whole earth is full of his glory.

HYMN [*congregation*]:

The ocean's vast abysses
In one grand psalm record
The deep mysterious counsels
And mercies of the Lord;

49

The icy waves of winter
  Are thundering on the strand;
E'en grief's chill stream is guided
  By God's all-gracious hand.

The starry hosts are singing
  Through all the light-strewn sky
Of God's majestic temple
  And palace-courts on high;
When in these outer chambers,
  Such glory gilds the night,
What the transcendent brightness
  Of God's eternal light!

Act Two

BLACK CHOIR:

What is mirrored in the silver brook?
Black night . . .
The star ripens on the branch.
Who is crying in the wind,
climbing up the tree,
rustling in the leaves?
The clouds are drifting, the star is falling

Beautiful brook,
where are you running
in the black night?
A golden ring, gleaming under root;
gleaming eye, gleaming in the hole.
In the black night
where are you running,
beautiful brook?

The clouds are drifting, the star is falling.
Who is rustling in the leaves,
climbing up the tree,
crying in the wind?
The star ripens on the branch.
Black night . . .
What is mirrored in the silver brook?

ISA: Beautiful, beautiful brook!

51

BLACK CHOIR: Black night. The star ripens on the branch.

ISA: No, I cannot see you any more.

BLACK CHOIR: Who is crying in the wind, climbing up the tree, rustling in the leaves?

ISA: Is it a star or an eye?

BLACK CHOIR: The clouds are drifting, the star is falling.

ISA: Beautiful brook, where are you running?

BLACK CHOIR: Black night, golden ring gleaming under root.

ISA [*trying to take something from the floor*]: Nothing!

BLACK CHOIR: Gleaming eye, gleaming in the hole.

ISA: Come out now!

SATAN: Do you mean me?

ISA: Oh, are you here?

SATAN: Where else?

ISA: I have the feeling—that you are everywhere.

SATAN: What do you want from me?

ISA: From you? Nothing. I was looking for the silver brook.

SATAN: And for the star?

ISA: For the star?

SATAN: To own a star. To hold a world in one's hand. Even to throw it away. If one desires one can throw it away like a glittering stone over still waters.

ISA: I never have dreams like that.

SATAN: But you might.

ISA: How can you hold a star in your hand? A star?

SATAN: Did you not see it growing on the tree of knowledge?

ISA: Yes, sometimes all stars look like the apples on the tall trees in paradise.

SATAN: Hath God said: "You shall not eat of every tree of the garden"?

ISA: Oh, no—we may eat of almost all of them.

SATAN: But on one of them grows a star.

ISA: God said: "You shall not eat of it, neither shall you touch it." But there are apples on that tree.

SATAN: And one of them is a star.

ISA: God said that one dies from them.

SATAN: Surely not.

BLACK CHOIR:
> Surely we shall not die—
> Hath God said—
> hath God meant—
> flowers of menace, skull,
> scare and empty shells—
> hath God said—
> hath God meant—
> surely we shall not die.

ISA: Do you really mean that a star grew on that tree? —Now I can't see it any longer, nor can I see the silver brook.

SATAN: God knows that as soon as you eat of it, your eyes will be opened.

ISA: So we can see in the dark—like tigers?

SATAN: You shall be as God.

ISA: But we already are, Adam says, because we love.

SATAN: A love without eyes. Blind fish stay in their

grottos, but the ocean and freedom awaits those who follow the light.

Isa: What is freedom?

Satan: To own. To own a star.

Black Choir: Or the whole world. Like God.

White Choir: What profits it a man?

Isa: But why has he forbidden us then?

Satan: To let you act differently. To give you your sight. To let you grasp your freedom.

White Choir: Through dwelling in love.

Satan: What good is it to be loved by the blind?

Isa: Look, it is gleaming—the beautiful animal.

Satan: The star is also gleaming.

Isa: Is that why you are called the angel of light?

Black Choir:

O darkness where stars are seen!
White angels, children of evil,
what do you know of heaven?
Who knows what is whiter than snow
but the sin more red than blood?
O Lucifer! O hell!
you alone know what salvation is,
in darkness where stars are seen.

White Choir:

What communion has light with darkness?
What is knowing without being . . .
No bridge or message,
no stars, only firebrands of self-destruction.
Though I have all knowledge and have not charity,
I am nothing, nothing, nothing.

54

IsA: The beautiful animal is still gleaming.

SATAN: And the star.

IsA: If only Adam were here . . .

SATAN: You call that freedom—you call that love? To look around for him when responsibility casts its shadow?

IsA: But why me, just me?

SATAN: Because you know more about being bound. Because the crown of stars is yours. And you see already—the very first creature on earth who sees.

IsA: I see the tree that it is good for food.

SATAN: Why then was it forbidden?

IsA: And it is pleasant to the eyes.

SATAN: What have you been using them for?

IsA: And it is a tree to be desired.

SATAN: To know, to know as God knows.

IsA: Its secret is a silence around it. Yet all the leaves rustle its riddle.

BLACK CHOIR:

> Now bursts the membrane of self-evidence . . .
> and red was never so red . . .
> and black was never so black . . .
> and the night has ribbons of blood.
> Look, cosmos of fire and darkness,
> heaven and earth a fruit in my hand,
> freed from its withering petal-bowl.
> Now bursts the membrane of self-evidence.

SATAN: You swallow. Your mouth is watering.

55

Isa: No, no, I don't want to. It is not true that I do. It is just the animal, the beautiful animal, that looks at me so that I see only the tree.

Satan: It is too late, my friend. You have already eaten it with your eyes, tasted it with your soul, said yes with your body. Look, you are swallowing again!

Isa: Adam! Adam!—Why doesn't he come!

Satan: I told you. You want to make him responsible. You call that love!

Black Choir:
 The hand is already open.
 It knows well what it is to take and to own.
 The spider lives already in the palm.
 My fingers are his web.
 The hand is already open.

[Isa *presses her hands to her body.*]

Satan: Look! Your hands are hiding. They know that they have already done it.

[Isa *walks up to the tree and takes a fruit (extinguishes a flame of the minora). Frightened, she immediately tries to put it back.*]

Satan: It is useless. It will never again grow on the tree. You have taken it; what is done is done.

Isa: But I don't want to eat it.

Satan: You don't?

Isa: But God said . . .

Satan: Did he not also say: "Neither shall ye touch"?

Isa: Yes, he did.

Satan: So you are already condemned, my friend; you shall die.

56

Isa: Die the death?

Satan: And should you have risked so much for nothing? Should you be punished without even eating the fruit?

Isa: But you said, "Surely you shall not die." You did!

Satan: Did I? But what did he say? And now that you know that you must die—now you know what it is to live.

Isa: Do I?

Satan: Hurry, before it is too late.

[Isa *takes the fruit with both hands and eats it. An* Angel *extinguishes the candle on the north side of the altar.*]

Black Choir:

What is mirrored in the silver brook?
Black night . . .
The star ripens on the branch.
Who is crying in the wind,
climbing up the tree,
rustling in the leaves?
The clouds are drifting, the star is falling.

Beautiful brook,
where are you running
in the black night?
A golden ring, gleaming under root;
gleaming eye, gleaming in the hole.
In the black night
where are you running,
beautiful brook?

The clouds are drifting, the star is falling.
Who is rustling in the leaves,
climbing up the tree,
crying in the wind?
The star ripens on the branch.
Black night . . .
What is mirrored in the silver brook?

ADAM: Isa, where are you?

WHITE CHOIR: What proximity could decrease the distance?

ADAM: The distance?

WHITE CHOIR: It increases as you approach.

ADAM: Neither angels nor principalities shall be able to separate us.

WHITE CHOIR: What communion has light with darkness?

ADAM: Into what crevice has she fallen?

WHITE CHOIR: Where the fire never goes out.

ADAM: Isa!

ISA: Here I am.

ADAM: Isa!

ISA: Are you blind?

ADAM: Here you are, and here I am. And yet I was closer to you when I was away.

WHITE CHOIR: Between us there is a great gulf fixed.

ADAM: What is it, Isa?

ISA: How could I know?

[ADAM *discovers the serpent and the eaten apple.*]

58

ADAM: Serpent!

WHITE CHOIR: Leviathan!

ISA: The serpent beguiled me.

ADAM: You must not die!

WHITE CHOIR: The wages of sin is death.

ISA: Why must I die?

ADAM: God said so.

ISA: But I am alive.

ADAM: Are you?
> The sun no longer glitters in the well,
> her light is like dust on the waves,
> the big mountain, stone on stone
> and not a miracle.
> Why climb it when not even the rapids
> throw themselves into the depths of God,
> but merely do what they must,
> their noise neither praise nor fear.
> Isa, why did you spoil the golden banquet?

ISA: But why were you not here?

ADAM: Was the sun or were the stars of the night with you? The wind which gathered fragrance for your hair? Was God with you? And you ask why I was not here. Where else was I?

ISA: I am lonely.

ADAM: *(turns to the altar)*: Lonely?

WHITE CHOIR:
> In that land where the mountains look toward the
>   wanderer
> the pine trees see him in silence,
> the birds are still when he approaches,

59

and the grass has no message;
the stillness is mute between blue clouds
and when the storm comes
it is deaf to his cry
in a land without God
without hope
without a bridge between steeps.

ADAM:

Father, where is the woman you gave me?
Where is the road to loneliness?
If she ascends up into heaven,
if she makes her bed in hell,
if she takes the wings of the morning
and dwells in the uttermost parts of the sea,
I shall search for her without end until I find her.
Father, where is the woman you gave me?
Where is the road to loneliness?

[*During Adam's prayer, the* BLACK CHOIR *surrounds Isa and* SATAN *walks around her.* ADAM *follows this vicious circle, trying in vain to find an opening.*]

WHITE CHOIR:

The queen of paradise is captive.
The sun her garment,
the moon her footstool,
and the stars her crown
are in the dragon's possession.

BLACK CHOIR: In the dragon's possession.

WHITE CHOIR:

The queen of paradise is captive.
Her kingdom's farthest galaxy is trapped.

The secret closet of the castle is unlocked.
There is no refuge.

BLACK CHOIR: No refuge.

WHITE CHOIR:
The queen of paradise is captive.
The cosmos of things and thoughts round and
about her,
gliding scaly walls.

BLACK CHOIR: Gliding scaly walls.

WHITE CHOIR:
The queen of paradise is captive.
Who is to crush the serpent's seven heads
and who to break his circle of loneliness?

BLACK CHOIR: And who to break his circle of loneliness?

ADAM (*standing still before the altar*): What shall I do?
Hit him, wound him, kill him?

BLACK CHOIR: Who dares tear his armor from him?
Who dares split his jaws?

ADAM: I do.

WHITE CHOIR: God created him, Leviathan is his, and
wondrously is he made.

ADAM: You also created the woman you gave me and
wondrously is she made. Let me save her.

WHITE CHOIR: Not in the sign of the serpent in the
moss; not in the world's dance with him.

ADAM: But if I cannot meet him as he meets me and
wound him as he wounds me, what is left? Thy will
be done, but tell me how?

WHITE CHOIR: Except a grain of wheat fall to the
ground and die it abideth alone.

61

BLACK CHOIR: Surely we must not die.

ADAM: Is it thy will that I enter the circle of death and be choked by Leviathan?

SATAN: To what avail?

WHITE CHOIR: To break the loneliness. To love the world back to love.

BLACK CHOIR: There is no love after death.

WHITE CHOIR: Neither life nor death shall separate.

SATAN: And when you sleep forever—who shall own the being that is left?

WHITE CHOIR: He who loses her.

ADAM: I am ready.

[ADAM *enters the circle and stands there with his arms outstretched like a cross.*]

WHITE CHOIR: O Lord God, strengthen the man who enters the serpent's circle with empty hands so that he tremble not nor weaken but let love bring him out of his perplexity.

ADAM: Be not far from me; for trouble is near; for there is none to help.

BLACK CHOIR: Himself he cannot save.

WHITE CHOIR: Holy, Almighty God, help the man in his solitary loneliness not to doubt thy presence which no eye hath seen, but to hold on to thy promise and to believe steadfastly through all perplexity.

ADAM: I cry in the daytime, but thou hearest not; and in the night season, and am not silent.

BLACK CHOIR: He trusted in God; let him deliver him now if he will have him.

WHITE CHOIR: Holy merciful Savior, eternal God, help the man in the hour of death not to tremble because of what he is leaving but to hope for the things prepared for them that love.

ADAM: My strength is dried up like a potsherd; and my tongue cleaveth to my jaws; and thou hast brought me into the dust of death.

BLACK CHOIR: Behold the man, stricken, smitten of God, and afflicted.

WHITE CHOIR: Behold the man, who loves.

BLACK CHOIR: Behold God's absence.

WHITE CHOIR: In presence.

BLACK CHOIR: In judgment, in judgment. Behold the sinner! He shall suck the poison of asps: the viper's tongue shall slay him. Behold the sinner!

ADAM: I am clean without transgression.

BLACK CHOIR: Behold, he findeth occasions against me, he counteth me for his enemy.

WHITE CHOIR: And God's deeds should be revealed.

BLACK CHOIR: By the sinner's wages. For the wages of sin is death. Behold the sinner!

ADAM: Canst thou still hear me? If thou still art, then let this cup pass from me.

WHITE CHOIR: Tribulation endureth only a moment.

BLACK CHOIR: A day or a thousand years.

ADAM: Tribulation, loneliness, anxiety, death—I can endure them, but let the image stay unblemished and the crown be without flaw.

BLACK CHOIR: No, the light of the wicked will be extinguished.

ADAM: If loneliness were not condemnation and death no
more than death, but the wages of sin, my distant God
—the wages of sin.

BLACK CHOIR: Affliction cometh not forth of the dust,
neither doth trouble spring out of the ground.

ADAM:

Behold the morning stars despise me;
the hopbines turn away from me;
the flax-finches leave when I look at them;
the great mountain closes its face on me
who am set to rule over them—
who bear the wages of sin.
My distant God,
take away this mark of death;
take away the curse.

WHITE CHOIR: Therein is he hiding himself.

BLACK CHOIR: Therein is he revealing himself.

ADAM: Is there no other way?

BLACK CHOIR: Surely we shall not die.

ISA: [getting up]: Why do you hesitate? Curse God
and die if that is what you want. But don't do it for
my sake.

BLACK CHOIR: Surely we shall not die.

ISA: I prefer a living man to a dead savior.

ADAM: But the distance? This distance between your
loneliness and mine, is that less than death? You speak
as a foolish woman.

ISA: No one has asked me anything, not even if I want
this salvation you think you will give me through all

this agony and profundity. But now let foolishness have its say.

BLACK CHOIR: Surely we shall not die.

ADAM: Wisdom or foolishness, is there any escape from this viper's circle of anxiety?

ISA: If you want to be with me, why do you search for me among angels and demons? I am always at your side. And everything is so very simple.

ADAM: So simple?

[ISA *hands him the apple.*]

ADAM: To live your life and to live in your world. But God? Our Father said . . .

ISA: Did not God say that a man shall leave his father and his mother, and cleave unto his wife? They shall be one flesh. Did he not say that?

ADAM: Think, if . . .

BLACK CHOIR: Might not God have intended this to be the sacrifice?

ADAM: To abandon righteousness.

SATAN: And so to learn the height and the depth of love. Cast thyself down!

BLACK CHOIR: Angels shall bear thee up.

WHITE CHOIR: Thou shall not tempt the Lord thy God.

BLACK CHOIR: Cast thyself down!

ISA: I will that you be with me where I am.

ADAM: Until death.

BLACK CHOIR: And the sin.

WHITE CHOIR: It is God that is love.

BLACK CHOIR: It is love that is God.

[ADAM *seizes the apple.*]

SATAN: It is finished.

[*Silence. The candle on the south side of the altar is
extinguished. Purple hangings are hung over the white
ones.* ADAM *and* ISA *turn away from each other.*]

WHITE CHOIR:
> This is the condemnation,
> that light is come into the world,
> and men loved darkness rather than light...
> The joy of our heart is ceased;
> our dance is turned into mourning.
> The crown is falling from our head:
> woe unto us, that we have sinned!
> For this our heart is faint;
> for these things our eyes are dim.
> Because of the mountain of Zion, which is desolate,
> the foxes walk upon it.
> Wherefore dost thou forget us for ever,
> and forsake us so long a time?
> Turn thou us unto thee, O Lord,
> and we shall be turned;
> renew our days as of old.
> This is the condemnation,
> that light is come into the world,
> and men loved darkness rather than light.

HYMN [*congregation*]:
> Thy word is like a flaming sword,
>   A wedge that cleaveth stone;
> Keen as a fire, so burns thy word,
>   And pierceth flesh and bone.

Let it go forth o'er all the earth
    To cleanse our hearts within,
To show thy power in Satan's hour,
    And break the might of sin.

Thy word, a wondrous guiding star,
    On pilgrim hearts doth rise,
Leads those to God who dwell afar,
    And makes the simple wise.
Let not its light e'er sink in night,
    But in each spirit shine,
That none may miss heaven's final bliss,
    Led by thy light divine.

Act Three

WHITE CHOIR: How long, O Lord, holy and true, shall we await thy judgment?

BLACK CHOIR: The day is coming to an end and nothing happens. Surely we shall not die.

WHITE CHOIR: How long, O Lord, holy and true?

BLACK CHOIR:
> Let him make speed and hasten his work
>   that we may see it.
> Let the counsel of the Holy One draw nigh
>   and come that we may know it.

WHITE CHOIR: How long, O Lord, holy and true?

BLACK CHOIR: All things come alike to all: there is one event to the righteous, and to the wicked; to the good and to the clean, and to the unclean.

WHITE CHOIR: How long, O Lord, how long?

[*Suddenly the angels of the* WHITE CHOIR *fall on their faces. The* BLACK CHOIR *turns away from the altar.* ADAM *and* ISA *flee as far from the altar as possible without leaving the chancel. Silence.*]

ADAM: I heard thy voice in the garden, and I was afraid.

[*Silence.*]

ADAM: I am naked. There is nothing to cover me.

[*Silence.*]

ADAM: I had to cover myself and so I hid in here.

[*Silence.*]

ADAM: The woman whom thou gavest to be with me—
yes, thou gavest her to me; I never asked thee—the
woman gave me of the tree.

[*Silence.*]

ADAM: That's why. The woman gave me of the tree
and I did eat.

[*Silence.*]

ISA: The serpent beguiled me. That's why. The serpent
beguiled me and I did eat.

[*The* WHITE ANGELS *rise and turn. They walk slowly
toward the chancel steps with arms outstretched, like a
white wall, driving out the* BLACK CHOIR, SATAN, ADAM,
and ISA, *until their wall of light stands like a fence across
the chancel steps.*]

WHITE CHOIR:
 A flaming sword keeps the way
 of the tree of life.
 The great dragon was cast out,
 that old serpent, called
 the Devil, and Satan, which
 deceiveth the whole world:
 he was cast out into the earth, and
 his angels were cast out with him.
 Therefore rejoice,
 ye heavens, and ye that dwell in them.
 Woe to the inhabiters of the earth
 and of the sea!
 A flaming sword keeps the way
 of the tree of life.

ISA: It is so cold and so desolate here.

ADAM: This is the land where the mountains turn around after the wanderer.

WHITE CHOIR: The pine trees look at him in silence.

ISA: The birds become still when he approaches and the grass has no message.

ADAM: The quietness is mute between blue clouds.

WHITE CHOIR:
And when the storm comes
it does not hear his cry in the land:
without God and without hope,
without a bridge between steeps.

ISA: Loneliness.

ADAM: Loneliness.

WHITE CHOIR: The flaming sword keeps the way.

ISA: What shall we live on, Adam?

ADAM: The earth brings forth nothing. It bars man's way with thorns and thistles.

WHITE CHOIR: Cursed be the ground for thy sake.

ISA: Can we go home?

[ADAM *and* ISA *walk pleadingly up to the angels. The wall of white angels does not move.*]

ISA: Let us come in! We are freezing and this is no place to live.

ADAM: The foxes have holes.

ISA: And the birds of the air have nests.

ADAM: But man has no place to lay down his head.

ISA: All the stones are rough.

ADAM: And we are strangers to the stars.

Isa: The needles stiffen when we seek protection under the pine trees.

Adam: And the shade of the oak expects us to go on.

Isa: We long for home.

[*Silence.* Adam *springs toward the white wall, but is thrown back as by an invisible power.*]

Isa: It is too late. You can no longer break through walls.

Adam: Not any more?

Isa: And when you were able to, you hesitated.

Adam: But it was you who wanted it this way. You forced me.

Isa: Because I wanted you to stand firm, even against me —firm for my sake.

Adam: You should have told me.

Isa: It would not have been a temptation then, and you would not have overcome it—and I would have been alone, even as I am now. Perhaps I could have stayed in paradise on account of you, yet even if I had shared all its pleasure I would have been in outer darkness.

Adam and Isa *(turned toward the angels)*: O barricade where our prayers fall down like wounded birds, which never cease to try their wings!

Isa: Adam, that flaming sword—it seems to stand between you and me also. I draw near to you—that is pain, that is distance. The sword will pierce me!

Adam and Isa *(turned toward each other with outstretched arms)*: O barricade where our love falls down like a wounded bird, which never ceases to try its wings!

71

SATAN: What has been, has been. But I say unto you: There is another paradise awaiting you.

ADAM: Far from here?

BLACK CHOIR: A paradise in the west.

SATAN: In the future.

BLACK CHOIR: Surely we must not die.

ISA: Where we are never to be cold and hungry?

ADAM: Answer her!

SATAN: Have you not yet understood your power and divinity? They are your future and your paradise. If you be the Son of God, command that these stones be turned to bread.

WHITE CHOIR: Man shall not live by bread alone.

ADAM: But paradise, paradise?

ISA: Who lifts the swallow from the ground without frightening her, tossing her into the sunlight over the spring-lake?

ADAM: Who builds a shelter for the doe when she is ready to give birth, and takes the splinter from the paw of the lynx?

ISA: Who helps the climbing rose to shape its arch, and turns the root aside where the parasol-mushroom shoots up?

ADAM: Who distinguishes between the grasses and gives a name to every kind of daisy?

SATAN: Don't you know that the new paradise will also be a garden? The difference is that you must create it yourself.

ADAM: Must I create it? But you said that it already exists.

SATAN: Yes, it does exist. In the future, in the west. And in you. I could show it to you before we go.

ADAM: Where, where?

SATAN: Here! *(He turns over a stone in pantomime.)* Under this stone, look—!

WHITE CHOIR: I saw a star fall from heaven unto the earth and to him was given the key of the bottomless pit.

ADAM: I see only ants and worms.

SATAN: Iron-legged, greedy tarantulas.

BLACK CHOIR: The gold of that land is good.

SATAN: Beetles, black and scarlet. Listen to their speed, rustling against the ground. They walk in line like ants, and pearl-glittering, deep down under the shimmering surface are the eyes of a man.

BLACK CHOIR: The eyes of a man.

SATAN: Some carry a sting, gray larvae, steel gray, and move their feet like iron hoops.

BLACK CHOIR: With a rustle as from chariots.

SATAN: On their backs, a little house like a shell. Look, in this opening for air and light—far within it—the eyes of a man.

BLACK CHOIR: The eyes of a man.

SATAN: And when the insect evolves, it grows wings.

BLACK CHOIR: They rage over the mountain tops.

WHITE CHOIR: At their sight anxiety takes hold of the people, and the rustle of their wings is as the noise of many horses and chariots running to battle.

SATAN: Their faces are . . .

WHITE CHOIR: . . . like the faces of men.

SATAN: You hear, they know these things up there too.

ADAM: Are they human beings? Or larvae? Or black angels?

SATAN: They are insect-humans. Highly evolved human larvae.

ADAM: But what is this pit in the ground?

SATAN: A secret entrance, a sort of eyesocket. It leads right down to your brain where the future has laid its eggs.

ADAM: My brain!

SATAN: Didn't I say that you would become Godlike, knowing, owning. That is evolution.

BLACK CHOIR: Surely we must not die.

ADAM: Is it so that God created the world? Who was it then that laid it like an egg in his thought? Was it you?

SATAN: Ask the crayfish where she got her claws, or the scorpion who gave sting to his tail.

BLACK CHOIR: Who gave blood thirst to the wolverine, and opened the follicle to the ants?

SATAN: When you left his little idyllic pastoral in the east, the world here, outside, was already prepared for my laws and my thoughts. He knows them—he knew them while creating—and how could he know them without wanting them if the power is his?

WHITE CHOIR: God will rebuke thee.

SATAN: But isn't he also responsible?

ADAM: If he did not want them?

SATAN: Then the future is greater than he. He who thought it out. He who nourished it as a larva in his soul.

74

BLACK CHOIR: Until it got wings.

WHITE CHOIR: God will rebuke thee.

SATAN: First the wings shall be tried.

BLACK CHOIR: Towards the west, the west.

SATAN: Will you come?

ADAM: Why should I stay here at a keyless door?

ISA: Because I am here.

ADAM: But this greatness, this future . . . !

ISA: Go to your future! I'll remain here.

ADAM: But we are short of time, we must get there before darkness. Come!

BLACK CHOIR: He shall rule over thee.

ADAM: God himself said so, didn't he?

SATAN: And didn't he also drive you out of the garden?

ISA: What do you know of love, Satan?

SATAN: Didn't you see the insect-humans? Whole ant hills of them and they are going to act as if they had one single brain. It is said that the two shall be one, but I say unto you: The millions shall be one.

ISA: With no desire for a home! And is the point of fracture where man lost his unity never more to ache? You call that love! I shall always look back.

ADAM: And I shall always look forward.

SATAN: Follow me.

ISA: Adam, don't go with him.

ADAM: Suppose I wish to? I am going to rule.

ISA: Not over my desire. And not over the darkness in my womb. No insect-children shall grow within me.

BLACK CHOIR: Hail, thou that art highly favored!

SATAN: Thou shalt conceive in thy womb, and bring forth a son, and shalt call his name Cain.

BLACK CHOIR: Cain, Cain!

WHITE CHOIR: In sorrow thou shalt bring forth children.

ISA: Yes, in sorrow. *(She turns to the altar with outstretched hands.* ADAM *walks behind her, holding up her arms.)*

ADAM: Our children! Isa—our children. Blessed be thou!

ISA: If only they could have played in paradise!

ADAM: But we will create a new paradise in the west.

ISA: I shall carry them back.

ADAM: That might be a long way.

ISA: Not farther than between you and me. Not farther than to God. And one day, one day the white wall might relent. Not for me and not for you, but for the crying of a child.

[*Meanwhile the* BLACK CHOIR *walks up between* ISA *and the chancel.*]

SATAN: But the black wall does not relent for the crying of a child.

WHITE CHOIR: The dragon stood before the woman which was ready to be delivered, to devour her child as soon as it was born.

[ADAM *shields Isa from the Black Choir.*]

SATAN: For your own good we have to force the woman to be sensible. Think of your paradise in the west.

ISA: Do you think that is going to make Adam forget what is threatening his child?

ADAM: East or west—curses on you if it is true that it will afflict the *child!*

ISA: What do you know of love, Satan?

SATAN: Are you trying to break through the wall, Adam? From which side and in what direction?

ADAM: I know where I have paradise, and I know where I have you.

SATAN: But you don't know where you have yourself.

BLACK CHOIR: We are you, we are you.

ADAM: Are you going to protect Isa's child against death and the devil?

SATAN: Who will protect her against you? And you against her?

ISA: The child will.

BLACK CHOIR: Thou shalt call his name Cain.

WHITE CHOIR: And I will put enmity between thee and the woman, and between thy seed and her seed.

BLACK CHOIR: Thou shalt call his name Cain.

ADAM: Yes, she shall. But her name shall no longer be Isa but Eve, because she shall be the mother of all the living.

WHITE CHOIR: Of all the living.

ADAM: And one day it will be revealed which child of her seed frightens you into calling all your angels out to battle.

EVE: Be it unto me according to thy word.

[*An* ANGEL, *a member of the* WHITE CHOIR, *gives a lighted candle to* EVE.]

EVE: What shall I do with the candle?

ANGEL: As with a promise.

EVE: What promise?

WHITE CHOIR: The woman's seed shall bruise the head of the serpent.

[*The* BLACK CHOIR *steps back.*]

BLACK CHOIR: Surely we shall not die.

WHITE CHOIR: And thou shalt bruise his heel.

[*The* WHITE CHOIR *slowly makes the sign of the cross. The* BLACK CHOIR *withdraws to the north side.*]

SATAN: Did you hear? They give your son into my power.

EVE: I hear that my seed will accomplish what Adam could not do.

SATAN: But I shall kill him even as poison kills.

BLACK CHOIR: The wages of sin is death.

WHITE CHOIR: And the gift of God is eternal life.

EVE: If only Adam had loved!

ADAM: But he who shall come . . .

BLACK CHOIR: Better a living son than a dead savior.

EVE: A dead savior—can death endure so much life?

WHITE CHOIR: O death full of life.

EVE: Like the tomb in paradise.

WHITE CHOIR:
    Gorge of the ever-thirsty forests
    the tomb where God's well dies
    to give the world life in resurrection.

SATAN: It is not death alone that must persevere. No one shall blindfold your eyes.

EVE: So may the sword pierce through my soul.

SATAN: You call that love!

EVE: Yes, a love for all the living.

WHITE CHOIR: For the earnest expectation of the creature waiteth for the manifestation of the sons of God.

EVE: The cockchafer that flies over the lake and never
returns.

ADAM: The aspen turning yellow in a hot dry summer.

EVE: A fledgling fallen from the nest, lying naked in the
grass while cries pierce the air.

ADAM: The star which no angel wants for her crown.

WHITE CHOIR: For we know that the whole creation
groaneth and travaileth in pain together until now.

SATAN: Together, you said. But no one will reach into
his loneliness . . .

BLACK CHOIR: . . . more than we.

EVE: But then is he where I am? Within the serpent's
inner circle? And I am not alone in my loneliness.

ADAM: And I live, yet not I.

EVE: But you live in me and I in you . . .

ADAM and EVE: . . . in what is more than we.

WHITE CHOIR: In love.

EVE: And the bird does not fall to the ground.

SATAN: Did God not say that the wages of sin is death?
Can God make himself co-responsible and not punish
evil?

BLACK CHOIR: Co-responsible!

WHITE CHOIR: (making the sign of the cross): Co-responsible!

READER: God so loved the world.

[*The* WHITE CHOIR *kneels. Silence.*]

WHITE CHOIR:
>O depth of burning darkness,
>wellspring which bears the chalices of salvation,
>above the desire of broken stems,
>resting on clarity.

ADAM: Red bursting from humanity.

WHITE CHOIR: God's love, a wound in his side.

ADAM: And man burst into unity: loneliness is no more.

WHITE CHOIR:
>O blood of God that taketh away
>the sins of the world,
>red water-lily on the well of life.

EVE:
>The white one shimmers in the dark
>only sensed far from earthly shores.

WHITE CHOIR: O presence where distance is not distance . . .

EVE:
>. . . for the sake of the red chalice;
>waiting for the bride of the Lamb,
>crown of bliss.

WHITE CHOIR: White water-lily on the well of life.

EVE: I can see home, all the way home!

ADAM: But is there a way of getting in?

WHITE CHOIR: A new and living way.

EVE: I can hear the water of life.

READER: Let him that is thirsty come. And whosoever will, let him take the water of life freely.

EVE (*with her hand cupping the flame*):

O flame,
So I will close myself around you
as I listen at night:
Does the ice crack against the waves?
Do the mountains, bared of their moss,
shake in the bitter cold?
Does the sea toss in its cradle?
And do the other children sleep—
the sparrow, the horse and the buzzard?
I will close myself around you.

I rest on my elbow and listen:
A star glows in my eye,
angels from afar watch my regions,
the mother of all the living wonders—
Is there peace or is someone crying,
someone in the peaceful blue about me?

So I will close myself around you,
around you who are the light of all things,
the heart of space that burns
inside all things that are.

O flame within me,
I will close myself around you
and all generations.

[*The* WHITE CHOIR *lights the altar candles from Eve's and returns them to the altar. When the candles are in place the purple hangings fall. The angels open their wall and form two lines leading up to the two candles. With increasing volume they say the canticle.*]

WHITE CHOIR:

> All generations, all generations, all generations, shall call me blessed.

> For he that is mighty hath done to me great things; and holy is his name.

> And his mercy is on them that fear him from generation to generation.

> He hath showed strength with his arm; he hath scattered the proud in the imagination of their hearts.

> He hath put down the mighty from their seats, and exalted them of low degree.

> Glory be to the Father and to the Son and to the Holy Ghost;

> As it was in the beginning, is now and ever shall be, World without end.

>> Amen.

[ADAM *and* EVE *walk between the two lines of angels to the altar.* SATAN *and the* BLACK CHOIR *throw off their robes and join the* WHITE CHOIR.]

THE OUR FATHER

THE BENEDICTION

HYMN [*congregation*]:

> Of the Father's love begotten
>> Ere the worlds began to be,
> He is Alpha and Omega,
>> He the source, the ending he,

Of the things that are, that have been,
    And that future years shall see,
    Evermore and evermore.

O that birth for ever blessed,
    When the Virgin, full of grace,
By the Holy Ghost conceiving,
    Bare the Saviour of our race;
And the Babe, the world's Redeemer,
    First revealed his sacred face,
    Evermore and evermore.

This is he whom seers in old time
    Chanted of with one accord;
Whom the voices of the prophets
    Promised in their faithful word;
Now he shines, the long-expected;
    Let creation praise its Lord,
    Evermore and evermore.

O ye heights of heaven, adore him;
    Angel hosts, his praises sing;
Powers, dominions, bow before him,
    And extol our God and King;
Let no tongue on earth be silent;
    Every voice in concert ring,
    Evermore and evermore.

Christ, to thee, with God the Father,
    And, O Holy Ghost, to thee,
Hymn and chant and high thanksgiving,
    And unwearied praises be:
Honor, glory, and dominion,
    And eternal victory,
    Evermore and evermore.   Amen.

THE FIERY FURNACE

Players

Chorus, *including*:

FOUR BEASTS: LION, OX, MAN, EAGLE

SHADRACH   WOMAN *(Shadrach's wife)*

ABEDNEGO   DAUGHTER ZION

Others

CAPTAINS: GOVERNOR, HAMAN, MESHACH

DEMAS *(later a Captain)*

BABEL *(a woman)*

READER *(Pastor or Layman)*

SPECIAL CHOIR *(if desired)*

*The congregation makes the appropriate responses
at the conclusion of the first scene of Act One.*

Costumes:

The players may wear albs.

The marks of the Beasts ought to be indicated by banners or appliqués (cf. Revelation 4:7).

The captains wear black robes over their albs. Meshach removes his robe when he is imprisoned and Demas later puts on this robe.

Babel wears a red robe over her alb (Revelation 17:4).

Daughter Zion (who also represents the Virgin Mary and the church) wears a white or gold robe (Revelation 12:1), or she may wear a blue robe.

The pulpit and altar hangings are red, or according to the church year.

Prelude

[*Enter the* PLAYERS *in procession while the congregation is singing.*]

HYMN [*congregation*]:

> Holy, holy, holy, Lord God Almighty!
>> Early in the morning our song shall rise to thee;
> Holy, holy, holy, merciful and mighty,
>> God in three Persons, blessed Trinity!

[*The* PLAYERS *kneel before the altar.*]

> Holy, holy, holy! all the saints adore thee,
>> Casting down their golden crowns around the glassy sea,
> Cherubim and seraphim falling down before thee,
>> Which wert, and art, and evermore shalt be.

BEASTS: Holy, holy, holy.

CONGREGATION:

> Holy, holy, holy! though the darkness hide thee,
>> Though the eye of sinful man thy glory may not see,
> Only thou art holy; there is none beside thee,
>> Perfect in power, in love, and purity.

FULL CHORUS: Holy, holy, holy.

CONGREGATION:

> Holy, holy, holy, Lord God Almighty!
>> All thy works shall praise thy Name, in earth and sky and sea;

Holy, holy, holy, merciful and mighty,
God in three Persons, blessed Trinity!

[*The* READER *returns to the chancel steps and faces the congregation with the closed Bible in his hands.*]

DAUGHTER ZION: Who is worthy to open the book and to loose the seals thereof?

[*The* READER *buries his face on the Bible as though in mourning.*]

SHADRACH: I beheld the tears of such as were oppressed and they had no comforter; and on the side of their oppressors there was power; but they had no comforter. Wherefore I praised the dead which are already dead more than the living which are yet alive. Yea, better is he than both they, which hath not yet been, who hath not yet seen the evil work that is done under the sun.

BEASTS: Who is worthy to open the book and to loose the seals thereof?

MESHACH: Mine eyes do fail with tears, my bowels are troubled, my liver is poured upon the earth, for the destruction of the daughter of my people; because the children and the sucklings swoon in the streets of the city. They say to their mothers, Where is corn and wine? when they swooned as the wounded in the streets of the city, when their soul was poured out into their mothers' bosom.

CHORUS [*except* BEASTS]: Who is worthy to open the book and to loose the seals thereof?

ABEDNEGO: The city of confusion is broken down: every house is shut up, that no man may come in. There is a crying for wine in the streets; all joy is darkened, the mirth of the land is gone. I said: My leanness, my leanness, woe unto me! the treacherous dealers have dealt treacherously. Fear, and the pit, and the snare, are upon thee, O inhabitant of the earth. And it shall come to pass that he who fleeth from the noise of the fear shall fall into the pit; and he that cometh up out of the midst of the pit shall be taken in the snare: for the windows from on high are open, and the foundations of the earth do shake. The earth is utterly broken down, the earth is clean dissolved, the earth is moved exceedingly. The earth shall reel to and fro like a drunkard. The transgression thereof shall be heavy upon it; and it shall fall, and not rise again.

FULL CHORUS: Who is worthy to open the book and to loose the seals thereof?

OX: As his custom was, he went into the synagogue on the sabbath day, and stood up for to read. And there was delivered unto him the book of the prophet Esaias. And when he had opened the book, he found the place where it was written, The Spirit of the Lord is upon me, because he hath anointed me to preach the gospel to the poor; he hath sent me to heal the broken-hearted, to preach deliverance to the captives, and recovering of sight to the blind, to set at liberty them that are bruised, To preach the acceptable year of the Lord.

READER [*returns to the altar with the Bible and puts it before the cross. He says or sings*]: Thou art worthy.

[ALL *kneel.*]

BEASTS: Thou art worthy.

CHORUS: Thou art worthy to take the book and to open the seals thereof.

CHORUS:

We praise thee, we bless thee, we worship thee, we glorify thee, we give thanks to thee for thy great glory, O Lord God, heavenly King, God the Father Almighty.

O Lord, the only-begotten Son, Jesus Christ; O Lord God, Lamb of God, Son of the Father, that takest away the sin of the world, have mercy upon us. Thou that takest away the sin of the world, receive our prayer. Thou that sittest at the right hand of God the Father, have mercy upon us.

For thou only art holy; thou only art the Lord; thou only, O Christ, with the Holy Ghost, art most high in the glory of God the Father. Amen.

Arrangement of Players
for Act One

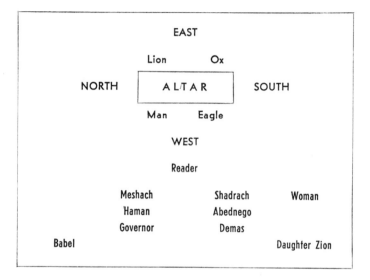

If there is a special choir it ought to be placed on both sides
of the chancel in order to make a frame around the action.

The "prison" is inside the altar rail, as is the "furnace."
Otherwise the church does not represent anything which
differs from a common service, i.e., it is the center of the
congregation and the cosmic scene as depicted in Matthew
25:31 ff. and Revelation 4.

91

Act One

The First Seal

THE CONQUERORS

HYMN [*congregation*]:

> For all the saints who from their labors rest,
> > Who thee by faith before the world confessed,
> Thy Name, O Jesus, be forever blest.
> > Alleluia! Alleluia!

> Thou wast their rock, their fortress and their might;
> > Thou, Lord, their Captain in their well-fought
> > fight;
> Thou, in the darkness drear, their one true light.
> > Alleluia! Alleluia!

LION: Come!

SHADRACH: Hear the word of the Lord according to the Gospel of St. Matthew. Jesus said: "All power is given unto me in heaven and in earth. [*The* BEASTS *fall down facing the altar.*] Go ye therefore, and teach all nations." Lord, what thou hast commanded is now done.

CHORUS: Worthy is the Lamb that was slain to receive power, and riches, and wisdom, and strength, and honor, and glory, and blessing.

BEASTS: Amen.

DAUGHTER ZION: It is all very beautiful. Only much too soon.

ABEDNEGO: But the gospel has been preached in all the world—even as it was written.

DAUGHTER ZION: "And then shall the end come."

ABEDNEGO: It is not too soon to rejoice.

DAUGHTER ZION: The birth pangs remain.

DEMAS: Does not the Scripture say that there remains a rest for the people? And that we shall press forward for the prize?

SHADRACH: A conqueror went out to conquer.

DAUGHTER ZION: And to suffer.

SHADRACH: Yes, in the time of the martyrs.

DEMAS: Nowadays all people speak well of us.

DAUGHTER ZION: Just as their fathers spoke well of the false prophets.

DEMAS: It is not easy for old people to adjust to the new times.

DAUGHTER ZION: The new times? I hear rumors of war and the very sounds of battle. These are the new times.

ABEDNEGO: One understands the importance of the church in such times.

SHADRACH: They say the war will soon be over.

DEMAS: Then the peace of the Great King will reign, the eternal peace.

DAUGHTER ZION: But where is he who fell into the hands of robbers?

DEMAS: The state takes care of him.

DAUGHTER ZION: God bless the state. And the inn between Jerusalem and Jericho?

SHADRACH: The Department of Public Health takes care of that.

DAUGHTER ZION: God bless the Department of Public Health. And the hundredth case?

SHADRACH: Which case?

ABEDNEGO: Which case?

DEMAS: Which case?

DAUGHTER ZION: You ask that. You who sing praises to my Son. About victory! But he said so.

ABEDNEGO: What did he say?

DAUGHTER ZION: That the love of many shall grow cold.

DEMAS: The governor is coming.

[HAMAN *and the* GOVERNOR *step forward, bearing a victory flag. The flag shows a red knight on a white horse, outlined in red on a white ground.* SHADRACH, MESHACH, *and* ABEDNEGO *bow.*]

ANOTHER KIND OF VICTORY

GOVERNOR: Who spoke of victory?

DAUGHTER ZION: I did.

DEMAS: It was theology, Your Excellency.

MESHACH: How nice. Did you sleep well?

GOVERNOR: [*looking condescendingly at Demas*]: The Great King declares that victory is won and Samaria is liberated. Who in the whole world can compete with his power? Now comes the peace which is without end, and the father of peace is honored by all nations, and kindreds, and people, and tongues.

94

DEMAS: We must sing the Te Deum.

CAPTAINS: Praise be the king!

BABEL: It is all very beautiful. Only much too soon.

HAMAN: But the will of the Great King is proclaimed over all the world.

GOVERNOR: And it is obeyed. A conqueror went out to conquer.

BABEL: And to be hated.

HAMAN: Those who hate him don't live long.

BABEL: Yes, in the inn between Jerusalem and Jericho.

MESHACH: Perhaps it would not be completely wise to let those prisoners die.

SHADRACH: May the Great King be loved by his enemies.

MESHACH: Is not the church paid to teach the Samaritans to love their enemies?

ABEDNEGO: But the dead do not love.

MESHACH: A word of reason from the church for once— if he does not mean dead in the spirit or Christian love or some other such mumbo jumbo. Even an amnesty could be defended.

BABEL: The dead do not hate.

GOVERNOR: It will be as the Great King commands.

DAUGHTER ZION: That does not calm me.

ABEDNEGO: Don't be afraid. The Great King is merciful.

DAUGHTER ZION: Merciful.

BABEL: I don't like their tone of voice.

GOVERNOR: They are not dangerous.

BABEL: But they speak of victory. Another kind of victory.

MESHACH: Yes, but it is a victory that exists only in their speech. Like their "king" and his enemies and their armies—they are as harmless as chess pieces.

HAMAN: Their preaching calmed a great many of our enemies until the Great King on the white horse could fall upon them.

MESHACH: The church has blessed our weapons.

HAMAN: What does it matter then if they chatter about their kingdom of heaven? Now that the Great King's laws are universally established, this dream will disappear.

GOVERNOR: Who needs heaven when he lives under the Great King?

THE HUNDREDTH CASE

CHORUS: Great and wonderful are thy works, O Lord God Almighty; righteous and wise are thy ways, thou king of the people.

DAUGHTER ZION: I hear a song. From heaven.

BABEL: She hears so much. That's her old age.

DAUGHTER ZION: A sinner has repented.

DEMAS: How many?

DAUGHTER ZION: Only one.

DEMAS: That isn't much.

DAUGHTER ZION: But it is the hundredth case. The one whom no one could help.

SHADRACH: And he is a Samaritan.

BABEL: Do you hear what they are saying? Is this Samaritan also theology?

GOVERNOR: What's the story with the Samaritan?

SHADRACH: He has received the forgiveness of sins, Your Excellency.

GOVERNOR: I don't know your system of merit and honors, but how do you dare give them to a Samaritan?

ABEDNEGO: The forgiveness of sins is not an order of merit.

SHADRACH: It's only given to sinners.

HAMAN: Apparently some sort of punishment.

SHADRACH: No—it is a pardon.

MESHACH: For imagined souls in an imagined hell with imagined punishments.

GOVERNOR: Could I, for instance, receive the forgiveness of sins?

ABEDNEGO: Yes, Your Excellency, if you confess your sins.

GOVERNOR: Sins? What sins?

BABEL: This is libel.

HAMAN: What is the difference, then, between the Samaritan and His Excellency?

SHADRACH: None whatsoever.

DAUGHTER ZION: My Son has given his life for both of you.

GOVERNOR: That doesn't interest me in the least. But I am interested in what you are saying about the Great King. Could he too receive the forgiveness of sins?

ABEDNEGO: On the very same conditions.

97

HAMAN: Do you think he needs it?

SHADRACH: Certainly.

GOVERNOR: And you say that in public?

DEMAS: Those who understand it are but few, Your Excellency.

GOVERNOR: A conqueror goes out to conquer and at his homecoming he is greeted by the church as an equal of those he has conquered!

BABEL: Shall the Great King pardon the Samaritans?

HAMAN: When the church makes them equal to us and tells it to all the world?

GOVERNOR: It might be misunderstood. As a deviation from the differentiated value scale for human beings.

MESHACH: But is it actually necessary to place so much importance on the opinions of the church?

HAMAN: If it is significant when they bless our weapons, then it is significant when they curse them.

MESHACH: Would the church really curse something so popular?

HAMAN: We have just heard that she does not curse the Samaritans.

DEMAS: The church will certainly amplify its liturgy according to your wish, Your Excellency.

HAMAN: And stop giving the forgiveness of sins to the Samaritans?

DAUGHTER ZION: Though their sins be as scarlet, they shall be as white as snow.

HAMAN: The foundation of our commonwealth is at stake—human inequality itself. I propose that the church be prohibited from having a say in these dangerous matters.

BABEL: And what has the Great King to do with Samaria?

HAMAN: If it turns out that many Samaritans are willing to share the forgiveness of sins with the Great King . . .

DEMAS: But this is just theology!

GOVERNOR: It looks more and more like politics to me. We had best observe the situation in Samaria closely, day by day.

HAMAN: Maybe their government will turn to the Great King for help?

GOVERNOR: It will be as the Great King commands.

MESHACH [to Shadrach]: This, then, is what the church has accomplished today: she has murdered ten thousand Samaritans with the forgiveness of sins.

SHADRACH: She cannot deny the reality of Jesus Christ.

MESHACH: The reality?

DAUGHTER ZION: O Lord of all mercy, have mercy on those who fall into the hands of men.

CHORUS [*and congregation*]: We beseech thee to hear us, Good Lord.

DAUGHTER ZION:

> The night the star was extinguished
> and you were taken from the straw,
> you felt the anguish in my hands,
> you were frightened by my consolation
> —don't cry.
> But behind us we heard the cry from Ramah.
> How long?

99

Is Rachel's wailing ever to be silenced?
Don't forget, for mercy's sake don't forget the least
    of these thy brethren.
O Lord of all mercy, have mercy on those who fall
    into the hands of men.

CHORUS [*and congregation*]: Have mercy upon us.

DAUGHTER ZION:

Think of their mother, the one who sees the stern-
    faced men approaching,
her children who must obey,
who must silence their hearts.
For thirty years I saw them come and then—
they had to blindfold your eyes,
otherwise, they would have never have dared;
but my eyes were always open.
Think of their mother and don't forget, for mercy's
    sake don't forget the least of these thy brethren.
O Lord of all mercy, have mercy on those who fall
    into the hands of men.

CHORUS [*and congregation*]: We beseech thee to hear
us, Good Lord.

BABEL:

My sons shall not hesitate
to brace with iron band
the tree that is split
so teaching the world the reality of Babel.

BEASTS:

Already the dikes of mercy quiver,
the people make noise and heed not the stillness of
    the three angels,

a cloud over the sea, black sail, the water whipping
   from stem to stern.
The windows in Babylon are hardly shut before an
   angered bull smashes the wall and the roof is
   thrown into the air;
the ground trembles when he rushes by.
The people stare after him on the mountainside.
The sea is clearing.
They go to dry their clothes.
Unseen, a rill then trickles through the dike.

The Second Seal

RUMORS OF WAR

Ox: Come!

HAMAN: Have you heard anything?

MESHACH: What should I have heard?

HAMAN: I didn't say anything.

MESHACH: What could happen in the peace of the Great
King?

HAMAN: Nothing has happened since the liberation of
Samaria.

MESHACH: What about the inn between Jerusalem and
Jericho?

HAMAN: Don't you know that it never existed?

MESHACH: There is a poem about it in the Health Department. The physicians call those poems case

101

histories. So I forgot that there is no inn and no prisoners and no prison doctors to be annihilated. Or to be remembered.

HAMAN: Pray that the memory of the tributaries is better than yours.

MESHACH: Why the tributaries?

HAMAN: I didn't say anything.

GOVERNOR: Can we talk here without being overheard?

HAMAN: It depends on how loud we talk.

GOVERNOR: The situation calls for a conference, immediately.

MESHACH: What situation?

SHADRACH [walks to the middle of the chancel, turns toward the congregation and reads]: Behold, I am against thee, O thou most proud, saith the Lord God of hosts: for thy day is come, the time that I will visit thee. A great nation and many kings shall be raised up from the coasts of the earth. Their voice shall roar like the sea, and they shall ride upon horses, every one put in array, like a man to the battle . . . The king of Babylon hath heard the report of them, and his hands waxed feeble: anguish took hold of him, and pangs as of a woman in travail.

GOVERNOR: Stop! Not another word!

MESHACH: Did he really say anything?

GOVERNOR: Did he say anything? Give me the manuscript.

[HAMAN *takes a manuscript from* SHADRACH, *in pantomime, and gives it to the governor.*]

GOVERNOR: Where did you get this information?

SHADRACH: What information?

GOVERNOR: What you said about the uprising.

SHADRACH: What uprising?

GOVERNOR: Don't act innocent. There has been no official word from the government about this uprising so far. Not even all the captains know about it yet. And you are already agitating for it!

SHADRACH: I don't understand a thing. Since the Great King forbade the church to have a say in matters of the state, I haven't even uttered a political word to my wife.

GOVERNOR: What was it that you just cried out to all the people?

SHADRACH: The word of God.

MESHACH: Has *he* ever mingled in matters of state?

GOVERNOR: There is no time for God now. Who wrote this?

SHADRACH: Jeremiah.

GOVERNOR: Is that an alias or his real name?

SHADRACH: Jeremiah is long since dead, Your Excellency.

GOVERNOR: But the uprising began last night.

SHADRACH: It began twenty-five hundred years ago.

GOVERNOR: What are you saying? You know that it is in my power to arrest you?

BEASTS: For the fierce anger of the Lord is not turned back till he has performed the thoughts of his heart.

SHADRACH: You have no power over me, were it not given to you from above.

103

HAMAN: It is not His Excellency who should be re-minded to give homage to the Great King.

SHADRACH: I wasn't speaking of the Great King.

MESHACH: Who, then?

SHADRACH: God.

MESHACH: But you said something about power, didn't you?

BEASTS: Of him and through him and to him are all things.

FULL CHORUS: The glory is his forever.

GOVERNOR: I told you we have no time for God now. Who are your contact men among the rebels?

SHADRACH: I was just now informed that there are any rebels.

GOVERNOR: And what are you going to do with that knowledge?

SHADRACH: Say prayers and intercessions.

MESHACH: Not much explosive power in that.

SHADRACH: And I will make inquiries at the Department of Public Health.

MESHACH: Go ahead.

SHADRACH: How is it at the inn between Jerusalem and Jericho?

MESHACH: Why do you ask?

SHADRACH: I want to rescue a few people, if possible.

MESHACH: Who?

SHADRACH: The wounded and sick of both sides.

HAMAN: He talks as if that inn actually existed. This knowledge is criminal.

104

MESHACH: Probably it has its source in ignorance of the actual state of affairs.

HAMAN: But he spoke of "both sides"—is that to be tolerated?

GOVERNOR: Wait a little. His measure is not yet filled.

SHADRACH: I don't know what you mean by criminal knowledge; the only state secrets I know, I just heard today.

GOVERNOR: From whom?

SHADRACH: From Your Excellency.

GOVERNOR: What state secrets?

SHADRACH: Those that have been hidden in this book until Your Excellency reported that they are taking place today.

GOVERNOR: What?

SHADRACH: That the kings have formed a conspiracy, that their armies are approaching; their voice roareth like the sea and the Great King trembles . . .

GOVERNOR: Arrest him!

[SHADRACH'S *hands are crossed.*]

SHADRACH: You are all witnesses that I was arrested because I read the text for the day.

GOVERNOR: The text belongs to the church, but the day belongs to the Great King. That is the dividing line and the church has overstepped it.

SHADRACH: I have read this same text on this same day for many years. And I did not know that today it was fulfilled.

105

GOVERNOR: Who else would know?

SHADRACH: Yes, who else? [*Looking at the altar*]: Who else? It is he who has stepped over the dividing line.

[*The* CAPTAINS *take* SHADRACH *to "prison."* MESHACH *examines his chains.*]

HAMAN: What are you doing with the chains?

MESHACH: They are real.

BEASTS: The word of God is not bound.

BABEL: He is silenced.

DAUGHTER ZION: Never did he speak louder.

BABEL: The prison has encompassed him.

DAUGHTER ZION: He has entered the prison.

BABEL: There is still time to repent and to take it all back.

DAUGHTER ZION: Suffer as a soldier of Jesus Christ.

THE IMPOTENCE OF SEALS

BEASTS: Madness of locks and impotence of seals!

[*The* CHORUS *divides into two groups.*]

    I. Where do not the four spokes meet?
        Where is not the world's nave?
    II. Where the wings of cherubim drive winds apart
        and their thousand eyes traverse dark space.
    I. O eternal focus everywhere,
        body stretched between four frightened horses,
    II. crucified on wind-rose petals,
        buried inside the twinèd nerves,

I. risen beyond man's mind and thought
     further away than the stars pierced upon the
     horns of the ox;
II. jubilant between the jaws of the lion,
     unreachable inside the bite,
     wounded bird in the eagle's claws, yet never
     pierced, the heart within his heart.
I, II. Madness of locks and impotence of seals!

HYMN [*congregation*]:

O may thy soldiers, faithful, true and bold,
     Fight as the saints who nobly fought of old,
And win, with them, the victor's crown of gold.
     Alleluia! Alleluia!

O blest communion, fellowship divine!
     We feebly struggle, they in glory shine;
Yet all are one in thee, for all are thine.
     Alleluia! Alleluia!

Act Two

The Third Seal

HUNGER

MAN: Come!

[*The* WOMAN, ABEDNEGO, DEMAS, *and* MESHACH *form a line before* HAMAN.]

BEASTS: And there followed hail and fire mingled with blood, and they were cast upon the earth.

DAUGHTER ZION: May God have mercy upon those who ordered it.

BABEL: He giveth the winds direction over the peoples, and the sky breatheth fire over their cities. He filleth the clouds with death and causeth it to rain over good and evil.

BEASTS: And the third part of the earth was burned with fire, and the third part of the trees was burnt up, and all green grass was burnt up.

HAMAN: A measure of wheat for a penny, three measures of barley for a penny.

ABEDNEGO: A whole day's salary!

WOMAN: And when we've bought bread with it, how do we buy our clothes?

DEMAS: We must pay the rent, too.

108

HAMAN: Citizens, these are but small worries; small worries now that freedom has been secured.

DEMAS: They say the uprising has been put down. Long live the Great King!

HAMAN: But of course the government supplies must be reserved for the King's loyal subjects.

ABEDNEGO: And who are they?

HAMAN: Everybody has the right to be interrogated about his loyalty in order to receive the mark of the King on his hand.

ABEDNEGO: So that's the new passport!

HAMAN: No one may buy or sell anything at all unless he is marked—as I am [*he shows his hand*].

ABEDNEGO: It looks like . . .

WOMAN: . . . six hundred and sixty-six.

[ABEDNEGO *returns immediately to his place.*]

THE CONDITIONS

WOMAN: Where can I get marked?

HAMAN: Go and get your husband.

WOMAN: I . . . I have no husband.

HAMAN: You are right when you say that you have no husband—because the state has seized the one you deny.

WOMAN: But I have children and they are hungry.

HAMAN: Unfortunately, your husband refuses them their share.

WOMAN: What can he do? He is a prisoner.

HAMAN: All he has to do is to sign a petition.

WOMAN: What kind of a petition?

HAMAN: Go and ask him. Next?

MORE CONDITIONS

DEMAS: I want to know the conditions.

HAMAN: I recognize you. You have made a good impression.

DEMAS: And the conditions?

HAMAN: That you confess your Babylonian faith.

DEMAS: The church has another faith.

HAMAN: But that's only theology.

DEMAS: Yes, but it is a different theology. You don't change theology as easily as you change your suit.

HAMAN: But it can be so cold that you freeze in your old worn-out one. And furthermore . . .

DEMAS: What?

HAMAN: Come and I'll show you.

THE SEA OF TEMPTATIONS

DEMAS: What sea is this? It shines like gold, yet it is neither morning nor evening. And its roar is like the roar of the crowd when it greets its heroes. It lifts cities up to the heavens on its waves and again they fall into the deep. But they shine in that short moment; they shine like mother-of-pearl. What sea is this?

BABEL: All the kingdoms of the earth and their glory.

DEMAS: Why do you show this to me?

BABEL: Because it belongs to me and I can do with it whatever I want.

CHORUS: For what is a man profited if he shall gain the whole world?

BABEL: He gains more than the world, he gains the queen of the sea.

CHORUS: And loses his soul.

CAPTAINS: That is only theology.

CHORUS: It is you, it is yourself.

CAPTAINS: Not much to lose. Remember what you might become.

CHORUS: A shell, a shell that is left behind.

CAPTAINS: A name, a name that is left behind—

CHORUS: . . . of one who committed treason.

CAPTAINS: Why speak of treason? With gold and glory you can serve the noblest causes.

CHORUS: What is high among men is evil before God.

CAPTAINS: Is bread evil, too?

HAMAN: A measure of wheat for a penny.

BABEL: And I? Am I not worth a theology?

DEMAS: But I must retain my convictions.

BABEL: You won't lack for them. The world is full of convictions.

DAUGHTER ZION: And void of wisdom.

DEMAS: One must go on living.

DAUGHTER ZION: Why?

BABEL: The dead do not think. But to live, to live with me?

HAMAN: Three measures of barley for a penny.

111

BABEL: Life for a day. For a month! To live for a month with the queen of the sea.

DEMAS: Thirty pieces of silver.

HAMAN: You shall not want.

DEMAS: I am hungry.

BABEL: He that cometh to me shall never hunger.

THE CONFESSION OF FAITH

HAMAN: Do you believe in Babel, the mother of all people?

DEMAS: I do.

HAMAN: And in the Great King, her greatest son, our savior?

DEMAS: I do.

HAMAN: And in one holy catholic state, the inequality of human value, the infallibility of the law and the immortality of meritorious politics?

DEMAS: I shall try.

[DEMAS *stretches out his hand to* HAMAN, *who inscribes the mark of the King on it.*]

ZION THINKS OF DEMAS AND
THE JUDGMENT OF THE POWERS

DAUGHTER ZION: For the love of this world has Demas forsaken me.

BEASTS: As a dream when one awaketh; so, O Lord, thou shalt despise their image.

DAUGHTER ZION:

    Should God despise their image?

    O Powers, O Angels, what do you know of him
        who sent you?
    Of him who cried for the city where there was no
        room for peace?
    You listen with cold hearts to the despair of money
        jingling through the temple halls:
    thirty burning pieces of silver thrown into the
        lover's hand.
    Where shall the lost child go? The heavens echo
        his steps into outer darkness.
    O Powers, O Angels, what do you know of him
        who sent you?
    Of him who cried for the city where there was no
        room for peace?

CHORUS: He was wounded for our transgressions.

ANOTHER TEMPTATION

WOMAN: Shadrach, Shadrach!

SHADRACH: My wife!

WOMAN: The children are hungry.

SHADRACH: Sell our possessions.

WOMAN: *We* are not allowed either to buy or to sell.

SHADRACH: Why?

WOMAN: Because of you.

SHADRACH: What can I do?

WOMAN: Sign your name.

SHADRACH: Deny?

WOMAN: Confess. Confess your wife. Confess our children.

SHADRACH: By lying?

WOMAN: Your truths have never given us bread.

SHADRACH: Can't the church help you?

WOMAN: The church? Has it ever understood any poverty but that of the spirit or any hunger but that for words?

SHADRACH: There are times when the truth is much more expensive than bread. It can't be bought.

WOMAN: Well, it's certainly expensive to me.

SHADRACH: It can't cost more than life.

WOMAN: Yes, it can. It can cost your love for me. You hate me.

SHADRACH: How can you say such a thing?

WOMAN: It's true. I'm keeping you from becoming a martyr with a good conscience. You hate me for that.

SHADRACH: Lord, how can this be your will? Why is your word silent within me? My heart is cleft and I have only half a faith. My soul longs for a word from you in a dry and thirsty land. My memory's well is empty. My eyes thirst for what is written but nobody offers me help. Your word is called living and powerful, but what does it say about this, about this?

CHORUS: If any man come to me, and hate not his father, and mother, and wife, and children, and brethren, and sisters, yea, and his own life also, he cannot be my disciple.

SHADRACH: Thanks, that is counsel, I presume.

DAUGHTER ZION AND
THE DEPARTMENT OF PUBLIC HEALTH

DAUGHTER ZION: My son said that and he always meant what he said. I am the one to know. [*She rises and walks to the woman.*] Let your husband alone and come with me. Maybe we'll find some bread. [*They walk over to the captains.*] Come.—Meshach, Meshach. Come out of your prison and act a little human.

MESHACH: I can't. The lives of many people depend on me.

DAUGHTER ZION: O you dried-up minister of ten thousand royal rules and regulations! Isn't it better to serve human beings than your beloved statutes? Look at this creature—and she has children who are even sicker than she is!

MESHACH: Has a doctor sent her to me? And does she have the King's mark on her hand?

DAUGHTER ZION: What did I say? If you don't give her something to eat I'll tell the whole city the truth about the Department of Public Health—the department which lets little children starve to death if they can't convince their father to become a coward, a lovable little servant of the Great King!

MESHACH: Hush, be silent, will you! [*To the woman*] What you need will be sent to you, but get out of here before anyone sees you.

DAUGHTER ZION: You are not far from the kingdom of God.

MESHACH: As long as you stay here I'm not far from the state penitentiary. Get out!

DAUGHTER ZION: God bless you, my son

MESHACH: Not too much, though.

DAUGHTER ZION AND THE POWERS

DAUGHTER ZION [*turned to the altar*]: How about those
  angels of which you spoke? Do they still behold the
  face of the Father which is in heaven?

BABEL: Angels!

BEASTS: For thus saith the Lord God of Israel, The bar-
  rel of meal shall not waste, neither shall the cruse of
  oil fail.

DAUGHTER ZION: But what are they among so many?

CHORUS:

> How long shall the wicked be permitted to destroy
>   the earth?
> His pride has poisoned the fields;
> even weeds cannot grow there.
> The olive trees yellow;
> we are denied their solace in the garden of anguish.
> It is hard to believe in the will of our Father
> when so many sparrows fall to the ground.
> How long shall the wicked be permitted to destroy
>   the earth?

DAUGHTER ZION: Why do the Powers remain silent?

BABEL: What Powers?

I WAS IN PRISON AND YE CAME UNTO ME

DEMAS [*to Shadrach in "prison"*]: My brother, why are
  you here?

SHADRACH: My brother, why are you not here?

DEMAS: Because I render unto God the things that are God's, and to Caesar the things that are Caesar's.

SHADRACH: So you render glory to God and criticism to the Great King?

DEMAS: Where is it written that one should oppose authority?

SHADRACH: It is written that we should love our neighbor as ourselves.

DEMAS: That's a strange interpretation of the Bible. I have read that whosoever resisteth the power, resisteth the ordinance of God. The ruler beareth not the sword in vain—isn't that how it goes?

SHADRACH: Yes, it does. And Paul was executed by that sword. Satan has taught that interpretation to many conceited authorities. Among them . . .

DEMAS: Shut up, for heaven's sake!

SHADRACH: Right. That's the way you serve your ruler. If you loved the King you would give him what he needs more than anything else—the truth; the bitter, undiluted truth. But most of all you love your own skin. Therefore you keep quiet about whatever does not tickle his ears.

DEMAS: And how about yourself, brother? You may have your private ideas about a Christian's duty towards authority, and if you want to risk your life so that you remain blameless and unimpeachable in your own eyes, then that's your business—

SHADRACH: Yes, it is.

DEMAS: —but there is dismay and consternation in the

117

congregation because you are so occupied with your own private brand of justification while your wife and your children are in danger.

SHADRACH: What do you mean?

DEMAS: Nothing that you don't already know.

SHADRACH: Then why do you say all this?

DEMAS: You know that, too.

SHADRACH: I wish I didn't.

DEMAS: You prefer to sit in peace and contemplate your little martyr's halo. You call that Christian love?

SHADRACH: O Lord, have mercy.

DEMAS: Shouldn't you have a little mercy yourself?

SHADRACH: And deny?

DEMAS: Deny your pride. Break the martyr's halo and return to reality.

SHADRACH: Which reality?

DEMAS: The Great King lets none of his servants go unrewarded.

SHADRACH: Get thee hence, Satan.

DEMAS: You have a stubborn mind but I'll pray for you. Farewell.

SHADRACH: Hear him, Good Lord.

FIVE VOICES ON THE DISGRACE

DAUGHTER ZION: What is it to suffer innocently, to be abused, as long as you are honored by your own people?

BABEL: But if the normal places of honor are scorned

118

and if no value is placed upon the traditions of Babylon —then there is always the calendar of the saints.

BEASTS: How empty is the ostentation of honor!

DAUGHTER ZION: Thou lettest Babylon rule out one lie with another, and Satan's angel smites our pride. Even the cold hearts of the powers are astounded by thy wisdom.

BEASTS: He catches the wise in their wisdom.

DAUGHTER ZION: But don't forget how difficult it was to suffer in that moment.

CHORUS: He was made sin for us, . . .

DAUGHTER ZION: . . . and spat upon.

CHORUS: He was despised and rejected.

SHADRACH: Hear him, Good Lord.

"I'LL FORWARD THAT"

DEMAS: [*to the woman outside the prison*]: Where are you going?

WOMAN: To my husband.

DEMAS: He is not allowed to receive visitors without special permission.

WOMAN: What shall I do then? May I write to him?

DEMAS: Perhaps I can forward your message.

WOMAN: I was just going to tell him not to worry about us. Someone has helped us.

DEMAS: Who?

WOMAN: Mary, the daughter of Zion, brought me to the minister of the Department of Public Health and we got what we needed.

DEMAS: I'll forward that.

WOMAN: Thank you. [*She returns to her place.*]

[DEMAS *goes to the governor.*]

HE DELIVERS THE MESSAGE

DEMAS: Your Excellency, I have a message for you.

GOVERNOR: Deliver it.

CHORUS: Their throat is an open sepulchre; they flatter with their tongue.

PROMPT ACTION

GOVERNOR: Meshach is accused of misconduct in office. Let him defend himself if he can.

MESHACH: Here I am, Your Excellency.

GOVERNOR: They say that you have sold bread to the enemies of the state.

MESHACH: I haven't sold bread to anyone, but I have given bread to some people. I don't know if they were enemies of the state or not.

GOVERNOR: Does the law forbid the giving away of barley and wheat, Haman?

HAMAN: The law has not reckoned with such an activity, Your Excellency.

GOVERNOR: So—a way to get around the law. Furthermore, they say it was done through the church.

DEMAS: Through conservative, irresponsible members within the church, Your Excellency.

GOVERNOR: Hence the church has mingled in the affairs of public welfare.

MESHACH: The church? It was just an old lady.

GOVERNOR: "Just an old lady," you say. I would rather encounter ten thousand bishops and church dignitaries than one old lady who has only her faith and goes on believing forever.

MESHACH: Does it matter what she believes?

GOVERNOR: You are living proof that the King was right to condemn the idea that faith is harmless to the state.

MESHACH: The damage done is minimal, though, Your Excellency. Nobody even knows her name.

GOVERNOR: That's the very point. If the church were an organization with well-known people for its leaders, then we could get at her, crush her or use her.

DEMAS: If Your Excellency permits me, I would like to point to a word by St. Cyprian: "Where the bishop is, there is the church."

GOVERNOR: I wish it were that easy. But she is where the old lady with the prayer book is. She might be anywhere.

MESHACH: What do you propose we should do, Your Excellency?

GOVERNOR: What we should do? There is only one person involved whom we know by name, title and address. You yourself.—Arrest him!

[HAMAN *seizes* MESHACH *and takes him to join Shadrach.*]

ZION, ASK YOUR GOD

DAUGHTER ZION: How can this be allowed to happen?

BABEL: Ask your God.

BEASTS: Could the Omniscient make a mistake?

DAUGHTER ZION: I am sure that you know the heavenly computation and you marvel at his arithmetic, but how will it all end?

WOMAN: Isn't he a powerful man and hasn't he many friends?

DAUGHTER ZION: Yes, but Babylon, how will it end for Babylon?

DELIVERANCE TO THE CAPTIVES

MESHACH (*inside the prison*): What a relief!

SHADRACH: Here freedom is five square yards.

MESHACH: But you don't need to tell a lie every time you turn around.

SHADRACH: Who forced you to lie out there more than in here?

MESHACH: An idiot, a cripple, a Samaritan. Whoever a doctor can save if he only lies.

SHADRACH: Lies about what?

MESHACH: This! [*Shows the mark on his hand.*] That I belong to that man. That I am his faithful servant. That I think his thoughts and judge people according to his damnèd law of the differentiated value scale for human beings.

SHADRACH: Last time we met you talked differently.

MESHACH: But I thought this way. Now I can say it.

122

SHADRACH: You think you are free to tell the truth in here?

MESHACH: Who can force you to lie?

SHADRACH: My wife, my children.

MESHACH: You haven't . . .

SHADRACH: No, not yet. I can still endure *their* hunger. That is the truth of my martyrdom.

MESHACH: Your wife has what she needs to live—and the children too, I believe.

SHADRACH: How do you know? Do you know them?

MESHACH: I was able to help them because I was living a lie.

SHADRACH: Thank God!

MESHACH: That I betrayed the truth? Be happy that you didn't have to do the same.

SHADRACH: Thanks be to God that they are alive, that they live.

MESHACH: Yes. Besides, it was on account of them that I ended up here.

SHADRACH: I'm sorry.

MESHACH: Don't you understand? My prison was out there. Your captivity attracted me the way freedom might.

SHADRACH: What did you know of my captivity? Or about the faith which brought me here? You have often mocked it.

MESHACH: Yes, because the church was words about words about words. A ghostly world of murdered truths.

123

SHADRACH: But isn't that how you captains want it to be?

MESHACH: Not I. Not since the Great King converted me to Christianity.

SHADRACH: The Great King?

MESHACH: With his differentiated value scale for human beings. I began to look for someone who said the opposite—and lived accordingly.

SHADRACH: And where could you find him? In the church, of course!

MESHACH: That was the first step. Someone read about the Samaritan harlot—and how Christ talked with her. And I thought: I wish this were true.

SHADRACH: Of course it was true.

MESHACH: Then came the second step—the ten thousand words—and I came to the conclusion that if Christ is true then the church is an attempt to neutralize him.

SHADRACH: Not the church! The church is the gospel. But we who are its children! I, Shadrach, who acknowledge a huge ego and a small faith, I am the obstacle of which you speak. We confess him and then proceed to usurp the role of the one we confess.

MESHACH: Yet—when I was weighted down in dread that perhaps Christ too was a myth, a point of view, a manner of speech (and what then was reality?)—then relief came through you. The truth.

SHADRACH: Through me?

MESHACH: They captured you. Then I knew that God was not only words about God, but that he is. The word was reality. It was iron.

SHADRACH: But if now all this is true . . .

124

MESHACH: It is true or nothing is true.

SHADRACH: Then the captains have opened the Scripture to us.

MESHACH: What does the Scripture say?

SHADRACH: [*turning to the crucifix on the altar*]: O weight of grace, not yet psalm or legend, . . .

MESHACH: . . . costly charms for golden chain, reward for captains.

SHADRACH: His back has counted the knots, his knees have weighed the green wood.

MESHACH: What element is heavier than suffering, brought together from all our centuries to one single day, a day of truth.

SHADRACH: Our brother then stumbled—the end of the line which the trailing beam has drawn upon our road, there they forced a man—he came from the fields.

MESHACH: "Forced," you said. To do what?

SHADRACH: I cannot say. Take the book and read for yourself.

MESHACH: "On him they laid the cross that he might bear it after Jesus."

SHADRACH: O weight of grace.

MESHACH: Reality.

HYMN [*congregation*]:

And when the strife is fierce, the warfare long,
    Steals on the ear the distant triumph-song,
And hearts are brave again, and arms are strong.
    Alleluia! Alleluia!

The golden evening brightens in the west;
    Soon, soon to faithful warriors cometh rest;
Sweet is the calm of paradise the blest.
    Alleluia! Alleluia!

Act Three

Fourth and Fifth Seals

THE PRISONERS AND DEATH

EAGLE: Come!

SHADRACH: What do you see?

MESHACH: I see my enemy approaching.

SHADRACH: Who is the enemy of a physician?

MESHACH: Who rides across the battlefield when all is calm again? Who comes over seas and deserts, hard on the heels of hunger? Someone should have seen his face, guessed his secrets, and harnessed his power in precise formulas. What happens when the physician is captive and the Great King decides the color for the scholar's lamp?

SHADRACH: The prison mouse is apparently not coming to call today. We ourselves may eat the bread we've saved up.

MESHACH: Don't touch it! The flies have poisoned it. The flies from the butchers' shops in Babylon.

SHADRACH: They have imprisoned us to save us . . .

MESHACH: . . . while death makes house calls in the city and the yellow army bivouacs in the villages.

SHADRACH: How long have you known this?

MESHACH: Do you remember the grass leaf we found in

the crack on the floor? We watered it daily with some drops of our drinking water.

SHADRACH: Finally it brought forth fruit, first the blade and then the ear and we broke our bread near it.

MESHACH: Just like having a picnic in the grass in summertime.

SHADRACH: We had our pleasure walking out there, wandering around in this cell, not saving our steps. It was five thousand steps to our blooming forest.

MESHACH: But one day the guard discovered you while you caressed the plant. The heel of his boot ground out the miracle of our prison. You hid your face in your hands, but I saw . . .

SHADRACH: What did you see?

MESHACH: Clouds between the bars.

SHADRACH: What did you see?

MESHACH: And I looked, and behold a pale yellow horse: and his name that sat on him was Death, and Hell followed with him.

THE ANXIETY OF THE PEOPLE

BABEL: Who is crying?

BEASTS: Woe, woe, woe unto the inhabitants of the earth.

DAUGHTER ZION: Where are the doctors?

CHORUS [*menacing*]: Where are the doctors?

BABEL: Who is crying?

DAUGHTER ZION: The church is crying.

BABEL: The church is dead.

DAUGHTER ZION: The plague does not come from her.

ABEDNEGO: The root of the plague is a lie in your heart.

CHORUS: The truth shall make us free.

BABEL: What is truth?

ABEDNEGO: Your captive conscience.

CHORUS: Where are the doctors?

BABEL: Who is crying?

DAUGHTER ZION: The church is crying.

BABEL: The church is dead.

ABEDNEGO: But not the word of God.

CHORUS: God's word is living.

BABEL: Her leaders are silenced.

DAUGHTER ZION: He hath put down the mighty from their seats, and exalted them of low degree.

ABEDNEGO: O land, land, land, hear the word of the Lord!

BABEL: Which word?

ABEDNEGO: Free the scholars, feed the stateless, love God!

CHORUS: Bread, health, peace!

BABEL: Crush the infamous! Silence the traitors! The people demand it.

DAUGHTER ZION: The people are in the churches.

CHORUS: Bread, health, peace!

COUNSEL IN THE NORTH

HAMAN: The people are frightened by the plague; they take their refuge in superstition. Something has to be done.

GOVERNOR: It has already been done. Demas!

DEMAS: Your Excellency.

GOVERNOR: Act!

THE KING INTERCEDES

DEMAS: As you wish, Your Excellency. [*He walks to the middle of the chancel while speaking to the people.*] In his deep reverence for religion the Great King has always warned against those factions that tend to counterfeit the teachings of the church for the benefit of foreign ideologies.

ABEDNEGO: Woe unto you who make white black and black white.

DEMAS: Under the influence of such reactionary attempts the church has weakened and become more and more alien to the religious needs of the people. The Great King has been worried over this development and has now decided to act himself and save the church. From this day on the church is not subject to any pope or council. The Great King is her shepherd.

ABEDNEGO: Woe be unto the pastors that destroy and scatter the sheep of my pasture! saith the Lord.

DEMAS: In the hour of need God has sent the Great King as a savior for the whole of mankind so that there may be one state and one church. Let us give thanks.

GOVERNOR, HAMAN, BABEL, and DEMAS: Hail to the King!

DEMAS: Since the King has appointed me as his representative in questions concerning religion, I hereby rule that his holy insignia are to be introduced into the churches.

ABEDNEGO: God shall smite thee, thou whited wall.

[*The* CAPTAINS *place the banner with the white horse in the center of the chancel.*]

THE TEXT FOR THE DAY

DAUGHTER ZION: What is the text for the day?

ABEDNEGO: When ye therefore shall see the abomination of desolation, spoken of by Daniel the prophet, stand in the holy place, (whoso readeth let him understand,) Then let them which be in Judea flee to the mountains: Let him which is on the housetop not come down to take any thing out of his house: Neither let him which is in the field return back to take his clothes. And woe unto them that are with child, and to them that give suck in those days! But pray ye that your flight be not in the winter, neither on the sabbath day.

DAUGHTER ZION: Something else?

ABEDNEGO: And he that hath no sword, let him sell his garment, and buy one.

131

THE TRIBULATION

DEMAS: Arrest him!

BABEL: Arrest him!

[ABEDNEGO, DAUGHTER ZION, *and the* WOMAN *withdraw to the south side.*]

GOVERNOR: Why hasn't anybody arrested him?

BEASTS: The angel of the Lord encampeth round about them that fear him.

DAUGHTER ZION: Not around all of them.

HAMAN: The state must have a list of his friends.

GOVERNOR: It has already been used.

DAUGHTER ZION: The night the star was extinguished.

BABEL: The Great King will find his way.

DAUGHTER ZION: We heard the cry from Ramah behind us.

BABEL: Why don't the mothers of my enemies go to sleep?

DAUGHTER ZION: What does the text for the day say?

ABEDNEGO: For then shall be great tribulation, such as was not from the beginning of the world . . . and except those days should be shortened, there should no flesh be saved.

DAUGHTER ZION: And when the Lamb had opened the fifth seal, I saw under the altar the souls of them that were slain for the word of God, and for the testimony which they held: And they cried with a loud voice, saying, . . .

CHORUS: How long, O Lord, holy and true, dost thou wait with thy day of judgment?

The Sixth Seal

COUNSEL IN THE NORTH

HAMAN: The people are worried, Your Excellency.

GOVERNOR: Those who have reason to be worried may be so.

HAMAN: Not even the dependable ones can sleep. It is the plague, Your Excellency.

GOVERNOR: Will it never end? What are the physicians doing?

HAMAN: They contradict each other.

DEMAS: Some want to seek advice from Meshach, the man you condemned to death. They have been arrested.

GOVERNOR: Go and ask him yourself. While he is still alive.

DEMAS: I am a theologian, Your Excellency, and I don't understand this.

GOVERNOR: Haman can help you. He is not a theologian.

DEMAS: But he is the Great King's captain. And to ask a favor of a criminal is humiliating to anybody.

GOVERNOR: But not to obey orders.

. . . AND YE CAME UNTO ME

DEMAS [to Shadrach]: Where is Meshach?

SHADRACH: He is asleep.

DEMAS: Does he know that he is going to die?

133

SHADRACH: He has always known that. You are going to die, too.

DEMAS: There is a difference.

SHADRACH: Yes, for he can sleep and you cannot.

HAMAN: Wake him up!

MESHACH: Is it the border police?

DEMAS: It is the King's captains.

MESHACH: Not much difference. You have helped many over to the other side.

DEMAS: He is sick. What's the point in asking him anything?

HAMAN: We have our orders. [*To Meshach.*] You can buy your life.

MESHACH: What life?

HAMAN: Look at this map. Here the path of the plague is marked. Right here the death rate is at its peak now.

MESHACH: Which death rate?

HAMAN: I am referring to the deaths caused by the plague.

MESHACH: Yes, the border police ought to know about that.

HAMAN: What do you consider to be the root of the disease? Where should we throw our resources?

MESHACH: Where the population is most dense and the malnutrition worst.

HAMAN: Where is that?

MESHACH: Your conscience ought to tell you. In Samaria.

[HAMAN *and* DEMAS *leave.*]

NO CROSSING

MESHACH: No crossing today either.

SHADRACH: You're longing for it?

MESHACH: Yes, but I'll do what Lot's wife did when she fled from Sodom. I'll turn around at the border. The earth is most beautiful there.

SHADRACH: You're thinking of what was crushed under the guard's boot.

MESHACH: I'm thinking of the rocks, too.

SHADRACH: The rocks?

MESHACH: That they exist, none quite like another. And how old they are, preserving secrets from the dawn of time. What nugget of gold is more beautiful? What star is more mysterious? I'm going to miss them.

POLITICAL ACTION

HAMAN [to the Governor]: Your Excellency. The source of the pestilence coincides with the resistance. [He shows the map.]

DEMAS: And the illegal faith.

GOVERNOR: I know. The value of the population there is extremely low.

THE EARTH IS DISINFECTED

HAMAN: We have tried to remedy the bad conditions in those areas.

GOVERNOR: How have you done it?

135

HAMAN: By forbidding people to send food packages. It has not helped, however; the population continues to increase.

GOVERNOR: But the ovens?

HAMAN: They have been used steadily—we lack no opportunities for that, since the resistance is so stubborn in Samaria. But in spite of all our technical progress it is not enough.

GOVERNOR: Maybe there is a solution . . .

DEMAS: The Great King's mission?

GOVERNOR: Perhaps one could call it that. One of the King's most fantastic ideas could now be put to practical use.

DEMAS: Which idea?

GOVERNOR: To burn them all up. Make a fiery furnace of the whole of Samaria.

HAMAN: But the smoke, Your Excellency. We have gotten many warnings against such fires on account of the smoke.

GOVERNOR: Our state scientists have declared those misgivings to be vastly exaggerated.

DEMAS: Will the King actually consent to such a—such an experiment?

GOVERNOR: Him? Oh, he will write the music for the performance.

THE EARTH QUAKES

DAUGHTER ZION: And I saw the Lamb open the sixth seal.

BEASTS: And there was a great earthquake, . . .

LION: . . . and the sun became black as sackcloth of hair,

OX: . . . and the moon became as blood.

MAN: And the stars of heaven fell unto the earth, even as a figtree casteth her untimely figs, when she is shaken of a mighty wind.

EAGLE: And the heaven departed as a scroll when it is rolled together; and every mountain and island were moved out of their places.

THE SPIDER WEB IN THE PRISON WINDOW

SHADRACH: What do you see?

MESHACH: The first spider of summer.

SHADRACH: In the prison window as always? There he encompasses the whole dark sky with his web.

MESHACH: He is catching no stars this year. The threads break easily; the great wheel breaks whenever a breeze blows around the cross-marked spider.

SHADRACH: Why does the bond break? Why do the spokes loosen?

MESHACH: Because the order is upset. The spider's egg is different, just as the whole cosmos is different. It is as you said: The great wheel breaks around the cross-bearing one.

SHADRACH: "Cursed is the ground for thy sake." Should the judgment fall on creation for a second time?

MESHACH: Whether it is judgment or sin—I don't know about those things. What I see is that man has worn away the thread that held his house together.

SHADRACH: "This is the condemnation, that light is come
into the world, and men loved darkness rather than
light." [*Looks up to the window.*] Iota loosens from
Chi, the forest's altar hanging is threadbare, and the
weaver has lost the pattern.

MESHACH: A damaged piece of art. A window with a
view toward a new world.

SHADRACH: What do you see?

MESHACH:

> The salmon swims diagonally up the river,
> with great effort the lark lifts from the field,
> ancient fir trees bear their crowns high above storm-
> fallen young wood.
> Which angel has now taken the torch-rose and
> bowed its flame down to earth?
> Like barbaric soldiers who roam through a
> conquered palace
> demolishing its art work and leaving only trash and
> dirt,
> so man leaves this house;
> bricks and billboards remain to litter the banquet
> hall.

SHADRACH: How do you know that there will be anything left? That everything won't dissolve and disappear?

MESHACH: That our world isn't going to melt down in
the fire of hell, you mean? How do I know—But if
there is a heaven and if sometime I am going to enter
it, thanks to the grace of God, I shall always miss this
earth. I shall long for night and day, for the soft
darkness when the bat spreads its wings, for the sun

138

which lures the viper to the big rock and hangs out pearls on the spider's wheel between the trees.

SHADRACH: And if heaven should turn out to be a new earth? If to die is the same as to resurrect? If the last afflictions are the pangs of birth and not the convulsions of death? And the flames in the fiery furnace are the dead bird's wings?

THE CHURCH READS INTO
THE SPIDER'S WEB

MESHACH: The place where all existence takes its leave and throws itself into God?

DAUGHTER ZION: For the earnest expectation of the creature waiteth . . .

CHORUS: . . . for the manifestation of the sons of God.

DAUGHTER ZION:
    Holy Cross, O promise in the center
    where the world is held together and the trembling
        threads meet,
    how long . . .

CHORUS:
    . . . how long shall yet the breaking cosmos,
    net of suffering,
    await its deliverance?

BEASTS:
    The hinges of the cardinal points are bending in
        powerlessness,
    the broken tapestry is flapping in the nightly
        breeze, . . .

CHORUS:
> . . . a banner with an emblem barely discernible, worn past deciphering.

DAUGHTER ZION:
> But it showed his initials, . . .

SHADRACH and MESHACH:
> . . . his secret seal on the cell's darkness, on our window to the stars.

CHORUS: For the earnest expectation of the creature waiteth for the manifestation of the sons of God.

ABEDNEGO DISTURBS THE PEACE

ABEDNEGO: Babel, Babel!

BABEL: Who is calling?

ABEDNEGO: The guard is asleep. The guard at the Great King's door.

BABEL: Who are you to say that?

ABEDNEGO: The shutters on the Governor's windows are not tight. His lamp has been burning all night.

BABEL: Who are you?

ABEDNEGO: Ask Demas, he knows.

DEMAS: There is no security.

BEASTS: There is no peace, saith my God, to the wicked.

DEMAS: Anxiety is rising in the city.

SECURITY MEASURES

HAMAN: Can't you preach to the people so that they will keep quiet?

DEMAS: The infidels do not come to the churches.

GOVERNOR: Force them to come and to hail the sign of the Great King.

DEMAS: In the churches?

GOVERNOR: Yes, in the churches. The banner in front of the altar shall no longer be merely a decoration. For security's sake let them confess their faith to the State. Let the theologians add to your beautiful preaching a few words on the divinity of the Great King.

DEMAS: Many people will hesitate then.

GOVERNOR: And we'll know who they are. Those who obey will make themselves hateful forever in the eyes of the rebels.

HAMAN: Start with the prisoners.

DEMAS: And Abednego?

GOVERNOR: His turn will come.

DEMAS: Why is he still free?

BEASTS: Thou shalt not be afraid for the terror by night; nor for the arrow that flieth by day.

DEMAS: What was that? Who sang?

HAMAN: Nobody is singing here. Steady your nerves!

DEMAS: We all need to forget Abednego, at least for one night.

ABEDNEGO DISTURBS THE PEACE

ABEDNEGO: Babel, Babel!

BABEL: Who is calling?

ABEDNEGO: The one you should not forget.

141

BABEL: Yes, I shall forget you. My feast is drawing nigh, my feast in blood and wine, and I shall forget you, I shall forget you.

ABEDNEGO: He who dances takes bad aim.

The Seventh Seal

SILENCE IN HEAVEN

DAUGHTER ZION: And when the Lamb had opened the seventh seal, there was a silence in heaven about the space of half an hour.

WOMAN: Why are the angels in the chancel silent? Why is there no answer beyond the four stars?

DAUGHTER ZION: Like the sound of many waters so was the praise around the altar. Yet we did not hear it because we had always heard it. Now when heaven is silent we say: "Why is it silent?"

WOMAN: It is also silent within me.

DAUGHTER ZION: It is the same praise and the same church.

WOMAN: It is as if a waterfall had suddenly stopped in its course and all the drops of water had frozen—like a veil hanging silently in the air. But why, why is heaven silent?

DAUGHTER ZION: Because of what is happening on earth.

WOMAN: What do you mean?

DAUGHTER ZION: The last things, after which there is to

be nothing else. What had to happen on earth will have been accomplished.

WOMAN: And what is left?

DAUGHTER ZION: Perhaps one sinner will repent, just one, the last one.

WOMAN: Who would that be? [*Turns to the congregation.*] Anybody here?

DAUGHTER ZION: And some will finish their course while heaven waits and holds its breath.

WOMAN: Shadrach?

DAUGHTER ZION: And you and I. We are many, I think.

WOMAN: But how will Shadrach hold out if heaven is silent?

DAUGHTER ZION: The word of God is not silent; it speaks on earth.

THE BABYLONIAN BANQUET

GOVERNOR: The day of the banquet is here and Babel has adorned herself.

[*The* CAPTAINS *and* BABEL *walk to the center of the chancel.*]

DAUGHTER ZION: And the woman was arrayed in purple and scarlet color, and decked with gold and precious stones and pearls.

ABEDNEGO: And upon her forehead was written a name with secret meaning.

CHORUS: With secret meaning.

DEMAS: Thus the feast begins—and this I say to all people, nations and languages: That at what time ye

143

hear the sound of the cornet, flute, harp, sackbut, psaltery, dulcimer and all kinds of music, ye fall down and worship the golden image that the Great King hath set up in his church and with one voice confess your faith in his holy majesty.

[*The* CAPTAINS *bring* SHADRACH *and* MESHACH *from the prison to the center of the chancel.*]

PARDON AND GRACE

DEMAS: In honor of this glorious day I have the privilege of pronouncing on you the Great King's pardon.

SHADRACH: How far will that pardon take us?

WOMAN: Shadrach, Shadrach!

DEMAS: However, there are conditions.

SHADRACH: I have the privilege of pronouncing on you the grace of our Lord, Jesus Christ.

MESHACH: Without conditions.

DEMAS: I don't want a grace which can be shared with all sorts of Samaritans.

SHADRACH: And I want neither yours nor the Great King's pardon if I can't share it with all sorts of Samaritans.

WOMAN: Shadrach!

DEMAS: We will see. The moment you confess your Babylonian faith the chains will be removed from your hands.

MESHACH: Why would we wish to lose them?

SHADRACH: Never have we worn more beautiful ornaments.

DEMAS: And why would you prefer to lose your life?

SHADRACH and MESHACH: In order to find it.

THE CONFESSION OF FAITH

DEMAS: In that case the two of you will be the beginning of the great festival, an example for the people of the kind of death he must suffer who denies the Great King. Because he who does not fall down and worship shall be thrown into the fiery furnace. [*A short pause.*] The hour has come. We believe . . .

ABEDNEGO [*comes forward, pushing* BABEL *to the side. He rips down the banner, throws it on the floor and tramples it underfoot*]: . . . in God the Father Almighty.

[ALL *except* BABEL, CAPTAINS *and* GOVERNOR *face the altar and recite the Apostles' Creed.*]

DEMAS: Seize him!

[*The* CAPTAINS *arrest* ABEDNEGO.]

GOVERNOR: Right into our hands!

ABEDNEGO: But now you know the wording of the true confession.

GOVERNOR: And you know the end to that confession. Now that we've caught you the others will also know it soon enough.

ABEDNEGO: What others?

GOVERNOR: Before we two are finished you'll have made several confessions.

ABEDNEGO: Of what kind? That the palace is surrounded? That all communications from this part of

145

the city are cut off? That our people have occupied all the roads around the city?

GOVERNOR: But not the road from here to the fiery furnace. Bring the prisoners over there and see to it that they get it seven times hotter than anybody so far.

[*The Captains bring* SHADRACH, MESHACH, *and* ABEDNEGO *inside the altar rail.*]

EVERYONE AT HIS POST

GOVERNOR: And now—everyone at his post to meet what is going to happen.

HAMAN: Are the rebels that strong?

GOVERNOR: If the Great King is surrounded then they are terribly strong.

HAMAN: Would they really be able to overpower him?

GOVERNOR: Never. But the moment they storm the gates . . .

HAMAN: What will happen?

GOVERNOR: You know what happened with Samaria.

HAMAN: Do they command such powers?

GOVERNOR: Not they, but the Great King does.

HAMAN: But if he is surrounded . . .

GOVERNOR: . . . Then there is a switch inside his chamber . . .

HAMAN: which would mean the destruction of the rebels.

GOVERNOR: Which would mean the destruction of mankind.

146

ZION, BABEL AND DEATH

DAUGHTER ZION: It is appointed unto men once to die, but after this the judgment.

BABEL: No one will survive me. No one will be left to judge me.

DAUGHTER ZION: God lives.

BABEL: Which god? The river was my god and a thousand roses fell from my gardens down into his bosom. But after me there shall be no rivers and Euphrates' star shall search for its image in vain.

DAUGHTER ZION: God lives.

BABEL: Which god? Marduch was my god, my god in the tower of heaven, in the wedding house, but after me the place for the cornerstone of heaven and earth shall stand empty. Where would Marduch live then?

DAUGHTER ZION: God lives.

BABEL: Why should any god live when I am dead? I who was the pleasure of the gods and the lily of the desert at the river.

DAUGHTER ZION:
    Why should you live?
    Your fires are mirrored on the river's surface;
    your pleasure yachts and war ships are trash and
        garbage, soon sunk, soon washed up on shore;
    your towers and spires are desert-stones on desert-
        stones, a place for the osprey to build his nest.
    Why should you live?

BABEL:

> To kill my enemies
> and to give the river
> a desert lily to love.

DEATH COMES . . .

BEASTS: Come.

CHORUS: Let thy grace come.

BEASTS: And this world pass away.

CHORUS: *Marana tha!*

HAMAN: Why is it so light?

CAPTAINS: The Great King's fire!

BABEL: His star!

GOVERNOR: His star in the east.

BABEL:

> No one shall own Babel after him,
> he has stretched his cosmic bow,
> an arrow of fire sings through my space,
> and the stake, a widow's pyre, shall shine
> through myriads of light-years,
> my death's immortality.

CHORUS: *Marana tha!*

BEASTS: For as the lightning . . .

DAUGHTER ZION: . . . and the distress of nations, with perplexity . . .

CHORUS: . . . the sea and the waves roaring . . .

DAUGHTER ZION: The heavens shall perish . . .

CHORUS: . . . and as a vesture shalt thou fold them up . . .

... AND THE JUDGMENT ...

HAMAN: There are four men in the fiery furnace.

DEMAS: Who is the fourth one? The one turning his back to us?

HAMAN: I don't know him.

DEMAS: But I do. Give my life back to me! Your Excellency, give it back to me!

GOVERNOR: Are you afraid?

DEMAS: I have betrayed innocent blood.

GOVERNOR: What do we care?

DEMAS: It is he, it is he!

[DEMAS *flees to the north side of the chancel. The* GOVERNOR *and* HAMAN *protect their eyes with their arms.*]

BEASTS: And heaven and earth fled from his face.

BABEL [*turning to the altar*]: Who frightens you? Another king?

BEASTS: Another King!

BABEL: And another glory?

BEASTS: Another glory!

BABEL: Why does the prison shine?

... AND THE GRACE

CHORUS: Jesus!

WOMAN: We are not alone in the fiery furnace.

DAUGHTER ZION: There shall be no more loneliness.

WOMAN: And no prison.

149

DAUGHTER ZION: So you have finally arrived.
The scroll lies open in your hand,
and the stars have exhausted their secrets,
all earthly joy is gathered in your eyes
and all the tears; O God, my God
nailed to humanity, crucified
to our thousand thousand years by Pontius Pilate,
now you have finally returned in glory,
and the earth burns in your bosom.

A firebrand is your mother:
you shall carry the old woman, you shall carry her
    home
to Nazareth, home to Nain,
home to what was love from the beginning
when the sparrow and the hawk played in the wind
and Eve asked the tiger to look after her children
while the great waters cried peace in her heart.

BABEL:
We who in this play have lent our voices to the lie
and brought it forth into your light,
we ask your truth to rest with us
and your creation born again in holy fire
to sing and play in our hearts.

[BABEL *and the* CAPTAINS *remove their robes and stand in front of the altar in their albs. During the following hymn the* PLAYERS *outside the rail may move in a dignified dance, holding hands, while the organ softly introduces the last hymn.*]

SHADRACH:
Praised be thou who created the heavens like a vessel
    of clay

and the ages like a bowl in your hands.
O potter and artist, may the artifice praise thee in
    the oven
and shine as a gem of fire.
Twelve pearls for the wreath of gates—
I saw the holy city.
Twelve stones for the crown of bliss—
that the bride may be adorned for her groom.
Twelve prisms—
that a thousand rainbows may dance in the marriage
    hall.

MESHACH *and* SHADRACH:

Praised be thou who so loved the dust,
strange plant from foreign shore
rooted in cursed soil,
tree of our pain with centennial rings
of peoples' anguish
and our evil barbed-wire blooming
in thy crown of resurrection in blessèd paradise.

SHADRACH, MESHACH, and ABEDNEGO:

Praise be thou, healing wind
over water:
storm stilled by the virgin's adoration—
Ave Maria!—
breeze burning in the world's center point
on a thousand altars,
fire-coal and wine on our unclean lips,
atonement.

BEASTS: Amen.

[SHADRACH, MESHACH, *and* ABEDNEGO *turn to the con-gregation.*]

151

SHADRACH:

>All God's servants round his altar who with open face
>behold as in a glass the glory of the Lord—it is time
>for the hymn of return.
>Unyielding Cherubim, cold-hearted Powers,
>glimmering flocks of autumn-birds, frightened by
>>his arrival,
>gathering on the fire-strings of heaven,
>sound your counterpoint.
>Milky ways and frosty crystals,
>lend the dewdrops purple color
>from your wings' mirror of the northern light.

BEASTS: Every knee should bow.

MESHACH:

>Now the harpoon shall understand its mission in the
>>white whale's heart
>and the nail its service in the wall where eels were
>>flogged;
>now the sunflower shall see the one for whom she
>>searched all day
>and the kingfisher dive for the last time to catch the
>>paradise-trout.

ABEDNEGO:

>Shine, O moon-lamp over the alpen lake,
>while the unicorn swims across
>and the hunter inspects the bloody tracks on the
>>shore.
>Lift, O white virgins, your lamps:
>mark with fire the road to Cana,
>because the cry is made . . .

BEASTS: . . . and every tongue shall confess.

SHADRACH:

> Be quiet, prisoners of the furnace, now breaks the bread,
> now the world staggers under his cross;
> slanted is the blood-ribbon in the chalice lifted up
> under downfalling skies.
> O words of institution!
> O consummation!
> O grain of wheat!

DAUGHTER ZION: Death is already melting away from God's acre, and the lark is bathing in the rainbow God promised to his harvest.

CHORUS: Jesus Christ is Lord.

THE OUR FATHER

THE BENEDICTION

HYMN [*congregation*]:

> But lo! there breaks a yet more glorious day:
> > The saints triumphant rise in bright array;
> The King of Glory passes on his way.
> > Alleluia! Alleluia!

> From earth's wide bounds, from ocean's farthest coast,
> > Through gates of pearl streams in the countless host,
> Singing to Father, Son and Holy Ghost:
> > Alleluia! Alleluia!

Amen.

153

Type: 10 on 13 Janson
Display: Janson, Vogue Bold and Erbar
Paper: Antique "R"